Lucky Mojo Curio Company
Forestville, California

✧ 2017 ✧

Vulvamancy:
A Guide to Yoni Divination and Magic
by Dr. Jeremy Weiss

text:
Dr. Jeremy Weiss

cover:
Cooley's Gardens Catalogue, 1972; Grey Townsend

interior artwork:
E. W. Alais; crop circle photo © Lucy Pringle, 1996
Robert Latou Dickinson; Grey Townsend

editor:
catherine yronwode

production:
nagasiva yronwode

First Edition 2017

Published by
The Lucky Mojo Curio Company
6632 Covey Road
Forestville, California 95436
www.LuckyMojo.com

ISBN: 0-9961471-3-6

Printed in Canada.

CONTENTS

Dedication, Acknowledgements, Introduction 4
Warnings and Advisements 5
What is Vulvamancy? 6
The Vesica Piscis and the Yoni 10
The Anatomy of the Vulva 18
Genital Modification and Mutilation 26
The Origins of Yoni Reading 36
    The Ananga Ranga 36
    The Perfumed Garden 38
A Complete Yoni Reading System 42
    Step 1. Read the Pubic Hair 43
    Step 2. Read the Labia Majora 46
    Step 3. Read the Labia Minora 46
    Step 4. Read the Prepuce or Clitoral Hood 54
    Step 5. Read the Clitoral Glans 55
    Step 6. Read the Scent 58
    Step 7. Read the Discharge 59
    Step 8. Read the Lubrication or Kama-Salila 60
    Step 9. Read the Female Ejaculate or Amrita 62
    Reading System Summary 63
    A Sample Reading 65
    Self-Readings for Women 67
A Complete Yoni Divination System 68
    Panty Divination 68
    Menstrual Pad Divination 69
    Ceromancy Pad Divination 72
    Bed Sheet Divination 73
    Fluidic Symbols and Their Meanings 75
    Sample Divinations 79
Vulvamancy in Neo-Tantra 80
    Vulvamancy in Neo-Tantric Yoni Pujas 83
    Part 1. Sacred Washing 83
    Part 2. Ritual of Reverence 84
    Part 3. Ceremony of the Reading 85
    Part 4. Rites of Touch 86
    Part 5. Blessed Love 86
    Part 6. Ritual of Union 86
    Part 7. Dance of the Divine 87
    Part 8. Bed Sheet Divination 87
Vulvamancy in Sex Magic 90
    Talismanic Sex Magic Ritual 92
    Cowrie Shell Vulvamancy Consecration Spell 93
Conclusion 94
Bibliography 95

DEDICATION

To The Reverend Bob Crow, who often quoted the wisdom of Dunninger, who said, "For those who believe, no explanation is necessary; for those who do not believe, no explanation will suffice."

ACKNOWLEDGEMENTS

Thanks to the late Ron Martin, a pioneer vulvamancer, for suggestions incorporated into this book. Thanks also to my colleague Julie Ann Johnson, to my editor catherine yronwode, to the original bed sheet reader and this book's production manager nagasiva yronwode, and to Greywolf Townsend for their contributions and their artistry.

INTRODUCTION

"Have you noticed how much they look like orchids? Lovely!"
— Robert Heinlein, *Time Enough for Love*

Throughout history, the essential teachings of genital readings have been scattered amongst various mystical and ancient works. It is an art that has been shrouded in mystery, due in part to social norms that imposed the use of euphemisms. Additionally, even when written down, much of this esoteric knowledge was difficult to follow, because without the use of drawings or scientific terms, it wasn't clear if the few existing bona fide practitioners of genital readings were even referencing the same anatomy.

This book is the first of its kind. In it I have collected all the known information, to which I applied correct anatomic terms in an attempt to standardize this long-secret practice. It has been a challenge. I have pored over texts, visited Greece, Malta, Turkey, Cambodia, Burma, and other exotic places. I have interviewed both women and men. I have consulted anatomy books and combed the current scientific literature. I have discarded what I found inaccurate and, when necessary, filled in the blanks with my own knowledge as a medical physician and practitioner of vulvamancy. All of the basic pillars of this complex art are covered within the pages of this book, which I hope will provide an excellent foundation for the novice vulvamancer.

I hope you enjoy the fruits of my labour.

WARNINGS AND ADVISEMENTS

The intention of this book is to stimulate and entertain consenting adults, lovers, couples, and the polyamorous, therefore the knowledge contained within should be used only between consenting adults and in ways that are consistent with your local and federal laws.

Vulvamancy should not be used for nefarious purposes, sexual or otherwise. It should not be used to defraud, manipulate, or to influence the woman being read in any way.

Never ever perform readings on children, adolescents, or minors; their anatomy is not fully developed and, legally, they are unable to consent to a vulva reading.

Never perform readings on non-consenting adults, the mentally ill, or the mentally disabled. This includes those who are incapacitated due to the use of alcohol or drugs.

Because the genitals are mucous membranes, it is also important to gently inquire about any health issues before beginning a divination. The use of gloves by the readers is a must for the protection of both parties who are not fluid-bonded. When choosing gloves be aware that some people are allergic to latex. If this is the case, there are non-latex alternatives and you should have them available.

At times the woman receiving the reading may need to have her anatomy adjusted in order for the genital reader to obtain an accurate understanding. In general, it is always best to have her adjust her own anatomy, rather than for the reader to do it. Essentially, try to adopt a "hands-off" approach. Some women are uncomfortable with touching themselves. In order to best navigate this issue, communication is absolutely necessary. Always ask before touching. Always let the woman know what is about to happen and why it is happening. For example, you may say something like, "As we discussed, your hood entirely covers your clitoral glans. I would like [you] to gently retract it so that I may continue with the reading."

Finally, strange as it may seem, be prepared for the fact that the woman herself may not know the proper anatomical names of her own body parts. Furthermore, many women have never even taken a close look at their own genitals. A chart may help.

Let caution, kindness, gentleness, honesty and humanity be your guide.

WHAT IS VULVAMANCY?

Vulvamancy is the modern term for a genre of divination that harnesses the unique power of the female vulva as an oracle. The current practice of vulvamancy can be divided into two broad practices of the mantic arts — character readings and divination. Both the readings and the divinatory methods of vulvamancy are complete methods unto themselves. They can be completely independent of other sexual, spiritual, and occultist practices.

YONI READINGS

The character analysis branch of female genital reading has a long history, especially in South Asian cultures. Because the vulva is called the yoni in Sanskrit, such vulvamantic readings are also known as yoni readings.

As with other anatomical character analyses, like palmistry, Chinese face reading, and the Burr Identification System of Br. Analysis (BISBA), the typical woman requests a vulvamancy reading to gain deeper insight into herself. She may be seeking self-knowledge in order to make changes in her life that will lead to greater happiness and satisfaction — or she may wish to clarify her own strengths, weaknesses, proclivities, desires, and dislikes.

Sometimes, the subject of the reading is not the client. In fact, the client may be a current or prospective lover or mate seeking knowledge about his or her partner. Such a reading gives insight into a couple's compatibility.

Couples may seek out yoni readings as a way to learn about each other, which can make them feel closer. The exercise of the reading itself can be a powerfully rewarding bonding experience.

YONI DIVINATION

Divination is the foretelling or predicting of events. Vulvamancers use one or more of four major methods to do this, namely panty readings, menstrual pad readings, ceromancy pad readings, and fluidic bed sheet readings. Bed sheet readings can make use of menstrual blood, post-coital fluids, amrita (female ejaculate), or a combination of any or all of these.

Divinatory vulvamancy can be done by a person of either gender, but as with other forms of foretelling, reading the future for oneself can be uncertain, so, if possible a professional reader should be consulted.

VULVAMANCY AND NEO-TANTRA

Tantra yoga comprises a loosely-allied set of Hindu and Buddhist rites set forth in texts dating from the 5th century CE to the present in which sexual union, either actual or visualized, may be included along with other practices such as the veneration of female deities and acknowledgement of the sacredness of the female body.

Neo-tantra is a modern term in Europe and the Americas to describe esoteric practices of veneration and meditation that, rightly or wrongly, claim descent from the sexual aspect of tantra yoga. The term is also broadly applied to non-Asian forms of sexual spirituality like karezza and eulis.

Vulvamantic readings and divinations have an assured place in Western esoteric sexuality. It should also be noted that Neo-Tantra includes and embraces vulvamancy's natural complement, phallomancy ... perhaps the subject of another volume.

VULVAMANCY AND SEX MAGIC

Sex magic may refer to any magical prayer, spell-casting, or contact work intended to bring about romance, love, or sexual pleasure. It may also include any form of magic in which a sex act like masturbation, intercourse, or the gathering of sexual fluids is a part of a work which may have as its objective not only sexual aims, but also non-sexual outcomes, such as curative health, psychic contact over distances, or even world peace.

Because the term sex magic is applied to so many forms of magic, there is no one agreed-upon way to integrate vulvamancy (or phallomancy) into magical practice. Therefore, consider these two quite different examples:

A sex magician might be asked to cast a spell on behalf of a female client for love-attraction, fertility, or curing. Preparatory to undertaking the spells, the magician might perform a vulvamantic reading on the client to determine what form the work should take and the likelihood of success.

A hoodoo practitioner who wishes to attract or bind a wife or lover might seek out a suggestively formed female-identified root or cowrie shell, dress it with his own sexual fluids, pray over it, and hide it in or under his bed. Employing vulvamancy on the variable vulva-shapes observed in naturally occurring curios such roots or shells would assist him to select the most appropriate curio to use in his own particular act of magic.

Fig. 1. Scholars and archeologists believe the vulva to be the earliest symbolic cave art. See page 10.

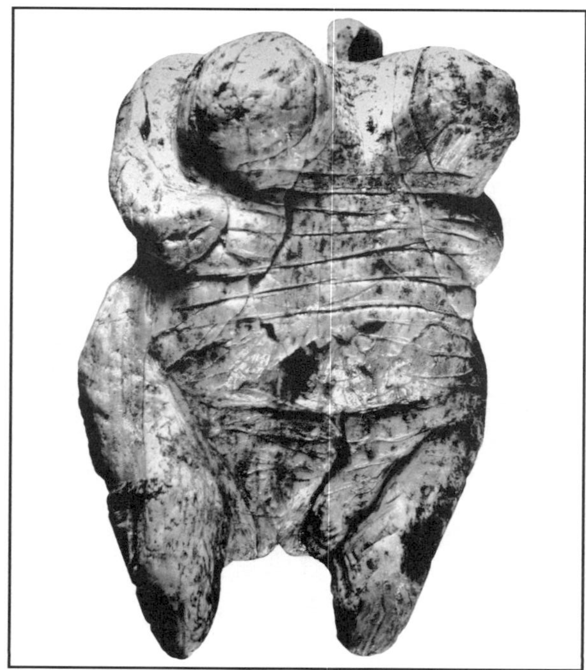

Fig. 2. The Venus of Hohle Fels, the earliest known sculpture. See page 10.

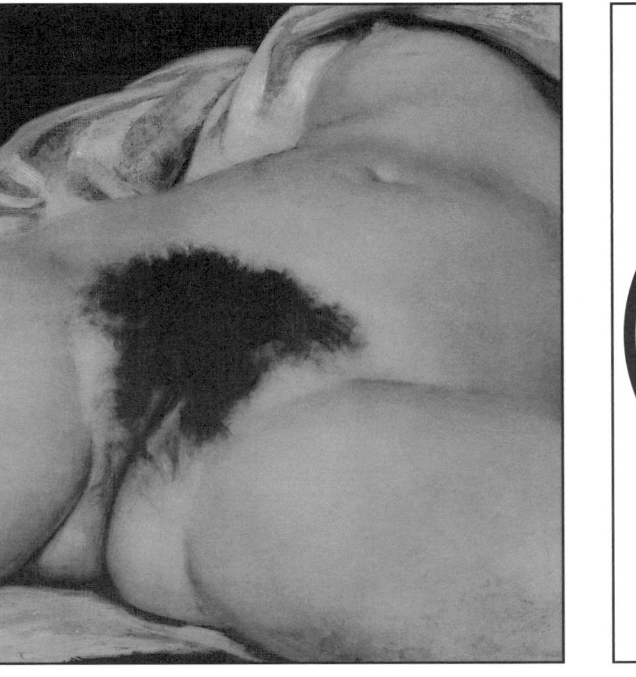

Fig. 3. The painting “L’Origine du Monde” by Gustave Courbet, 1866. See page 10.

Fig. 4. The geometric consruction of the vesica viscis from two circles. See page 10.

THE VESICA PISCIS AND THE YONI

To best understand the development of vulvamancy, we shall begin with a brief survey of spiritual and folkloric representations of the vulva.

DEPICTIONS OF THE VULVA

In 2007, a team of American and European archeologists excavating a site in the south of France called Abri Castanet discovered the world's earliest symbolic cave art. The team had been excavating a large block of limestone that had fallen from the roof of the cave. They broke the slab into sections so they could be more easily removed for study and, as they lifted the pieces, they discovered that the underside had been deeply engraved with images. These roughly 37,000 year old engravings were created by Aurignacian human cave dwellers. What was on the minds of these early hominid hunters? Was it fire? An animal? The sun? The moon? No. The engraved drawings were of vulvas. The vulva was the first known muse of artistic expression. (See Figure 1.)

The earliest known figurine is made from the tusk of a mammoth. Found in Schelklingen, Germany, the The Venus of Hohle Fels is a large breasted woman with a disproportionately large vulva. (See Figure 2.)

As an incidental note, *L'Origine du Monde [Origin of the World]* by Gustave Courbet, painted in 1866, was the first formally "realistic" painting of a vulva to be shown in a European art museum. (See Figure 3.)

THE VESICA PISCIS OR MANDORLA

When two circles of identical radius are overlapped but offset so that the center of each is on the circumference of the other, the resulting intersecting area is a symmetric lens. The Latin name for this shape, vesica piscis, means "fish bladder," after the similarly shaped swim bladders in fishes. In Italian it is called the mandorla ("almond"), which it also resembles. (See Figure 4.)

The vesica piscis appears in ancient astronomy as a representation of an eclipse. In plane geometry it occurs in the first proposition of Euclid's *Elements*, where construction of a mandorla is the initial step in the creation of an equilateral triangle. (The triangle's vertices are the two circle centers and one of the two points of the vesica piscis.)

THE VESICA PISCIS IN ART AND ARCHITECTURE

The vesica piscis is integral to an ancient symbol now known as the flower of life, composed of six evenly-spaced overlapping circles. This pattern can be enclosed within a bounding circle or repeated outward to encompass 19 complete circles and 36 partial circular arcs within a larger circle. It can also be continued endlessly as a tessellation, after the manner of arrayed hexagons. In all instances, the vesica piscis is the dominant figure within the flower of life. (See Figure 5.)

From 3000 BCE to 2000 BCE the ceremonial site Stonehenge was constructed in Wiltshire, England. In 2010 Andrew Monkman proposed that although no actual vesica piscis can be seen in the remnant stone-works, knowledge of its geometry was used by the site's builders.

A more clearly obvious early example of the flower of life pattern is the one engraved on a massive gypsum or alabaster threshold in one of the palaces of King Ashurbanipal at Dar-Sharrukin in Assyria, now northern Iraq. Dated to circa 654 BCE, it is currently on display in the Assyrian rooms of the Louvre museum in Paris. (See Figure 6.)

The flower of life shape also appears in the Jewish Kabbalah, where it helps to create the geometry of the tree of life, a mystical concept that forms a symbolical model of all reality, The tree of life is essentially the "cosmology" of the Kabbalah, in which the tree represents a "map" of Creation that is used to understand the nature of God and the manner in which He created the world.

It is interesting to note that many English crop circles utilize the vesica piscis in intriguing ways. In a 1996 crop circle with the shape of the vesica piscis, investigators reported that a terrific surge of energy could be felt while walking into the central mandorla. (See Figure 7.)

In 2005, the Trementina Base in New Mexico was revealed to the world. Albuquerque's KRQE-TV broke the story of a strange landscape marking in the remote desert, recognizable only from a high altitude — two overlapping circles forming a vesica piscis, and matching the logo of the Scientology-affiliated Church of Spiritual Technology. Despite the church's efforts to squelch the story, the truth came out: The enormous vesica piscis symbol marks the presence of an underground vault where the writings of Scientology's founder, engraved on stainless steel plates and encased in titanium capsules, are stored for all eternity. (See Figure 8.)

Fig. 5. The flower of life pattern, developed from tesselating vesica piscis elements. See page 11.

Fig. 6. The flower of life pattern in the floor of a palace of King Ashurbanipal. See page 11.

Fig. 7. The vesica piscis in an English crop circle, photographed in 1996. See page 11.

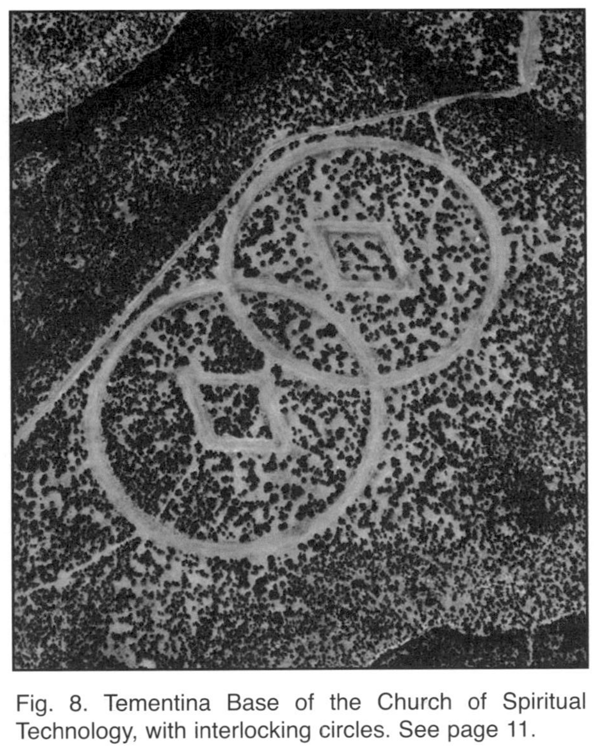

Fig. 8. Tementina Base of the Church of Spiritual Technology, with interlocking circles. See page 11.

THE VESICA PISCIS AND THE SQUARE ROOT OF THREE

Contained within this early symbol of female genitalia is a uniquely holy mathematical secret. The ratio of the height of the vesica piscis to the width across its center is equal to the square root of three (1.7320…), which is an irrational number (like pi). The sacred geometry of Christian Mediæval Gothic art and architecturemade extensive use of the vesica piscis and its association with this sacred irrational number, for the square root of three was a symbol of the Trinitarian Godhead. Arches in the form of a half vesica piscis virtually define Gothic architecture, and as religious symbols they are found in abbeys, parish churches, cathedrals, and chapels throughout Europe. (See Figure 9.)

The Gothic masons may not have known that the square root of three was comprised of an infinite number of non-recurring digits, but they knew it wasn't a rational fraction — and that was enough to convince them that it was God's number and not man's. It is interesting to note that the square root of three was so important to the Gothic masons, that Chartres Cathedral in France, with its many half vesica piscis shaped arches and windows, utilizes no squares at all; rather, the builders limited themselves only to rectangles with sides in the ratio of 1 to 0.86602540378, which is half the square root of three — a half vesica piscis.

The mandorla became the shape within which Mediæval European artists often enframed their mystical images of the Virgin Mary and Jesus Christ. Again, the square root of 3 alludes to The Trinity. (See Figure 10.)

With one end extended by a triangular shape to look like the tail of a fish, the vesica piscis ("fish bladder") becomes the ICHTHYS or "fish" symbol of the Christian faith. You may have noticed it on the backs of cars.

This fish bladder symbol also figures in the Biblical miracle of the fishes. The Gospel of John 21:11 reveals the number "153" — a number that appears in a mathematical ratio (265:153 = 1.7320…) that attempts to, but does not quite "solve" the irrational square root of three : *"Simon Peter went up, and drew the net to land full of great fishes, one hundred and fifty and three: and for all there were so many, yet was not the net broken."*

The mystical nature of the mandorla was also recognized by the Freemasons as a symbol of God and Geometry and it appears in the shapes of the collars worn by Masonic officers and as the bounding shape of the enclosures of the seals of Masonic lodges.

THE YONI

The Indo-Aryan and South Asian name for the vulva is "yoni," a word also translated as "womb." It may refer to geometrical figures, to ritual altar pieces used in goddess veneration, and to the vulvas of a living women. Additionally, the word yoni was picked up by 20th century Americans and Europeans who, either out of a desire to be courteously euphemistic or knowledgeably "exotic," applied it almost exclusively to the female genitalia, without understanding its further usage in South Asia.

The yoni (and its male counterpart, the lingam) first appeared as religious symbols during the Epic and Purana periods of Indian history, circa 500 BCE through circa 500 CE. It was in this era that two major and complementary Hindu religions — Shaivism and Shaktism — arose.

Shaivism is the name given to the veneration of the phallic god Shiva and local phallic gods such as Rudra and Bhairava as the ultimate godhead. A Shaivite god may be depicted as a human male with an erection or as a stylized or realistic penis called the lingam. Natural elongated stones, stalactites, and ice formations are also be said to be lingams. (See Figure 11.)

Shaktism is the veneration of local and regional goddesses, including Durga, Kali, Sati, Parvati, Sarasvati, Lakshmi, Mahadevi, and the Matrikas. Each has her own attributes, stories, and festivals, but most Shaktiite Hindus consider all goddesses as Devi (Goddess) or Shakti (Power), the ultimate godhead. The symbol of Shakti is a stylized or realistic yoni. Natural cleft stones, springs, and water wells are also said to be yonis. Veneration of the yoni, either in a mystical vision or as part of the body of a woman, has for centuries been a feature of tantra yoga, in particular, the practices of the kaula lineage. The most famous treatise on yoni veneration is the 17th century *Yoni Tantra,* which is framed as a discourse between Shiva and Parvati on the sacredness of the yoni. This text contains affirmations such as *"Women are divinity, women are life, women are truly jewels," "By worshipping the yoni one certainly worships Shakti,"* and *"All worship is pointless without worship of the yoni."*

The yoni and the lingam can be depicted and venerated separately, but Shaivism and Shaktism are complementary, and so the yoni and lingam came to represent Shiva and Shakti in union, both in the form of stylized lingam-in-yoni altar pieces carved of stone, and in traditional teachings in which maithuna (sexual union) forms a part of the worship service. (See Figure 12.)

Fig. 9. The vesica piscis in Gothic arches; the 3 of Pentacles in the Rider-Waite-Smith tarot. See page 14.

Fig. 10. The mandorla or almond shape in Roman Catholic religious art. See page 14.

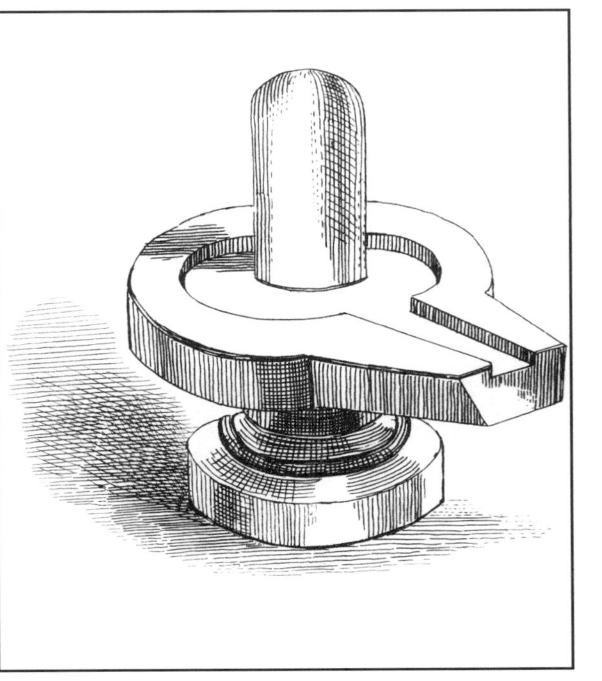

Fig. 11. Hindu lingam in yoni from *"Nature Worship"* by H. Jennings; art by E. W. Alais, 1891. See page 15.

Fig. 12. A 19th century carved wood yoni puja shrine from South India. See page 15.

THE ANATOMY OF THE VULVA

Like palm reading, yoni reading provides insights into a woman's major life events: birth, youth, motherhood, and senescence. And in the same way that palm patterns vary, so do women's vulvas. But before one can delve into either these lifetime changes and the differences among women, a review of the basic anatomy of the female genitalia should be undertaken.

Early attempts at vulva categorization and systemization were forward-thinking breakthroughs, but they lacked anatomic standardization and were rife with subjectivity. With neither illustrations nor agreed-upon nomenclature, confusion proliferated. For this reason, anatomic knowledge is the first essential skill needed to become an expert modern vulvamancer.

A copy of Robert Latou Dickinson's *Human Sex Anatomy* would be of great value to the serious student of vulvamancy. Dickinson, a talented artist as well as a medical doctor, made life drawings of the genitalia of thousands of men and women, noting the variations in size, shape, texture, and distensibility among his subjects. His gentle wit and evident wisdom inform this classic text in a way that mere photos cannot do, and the book is just as useful today as it was when first published, decades ago.

THE VULVA IS NOT THE VAGINA

The visible external female sexual genitalia is known as the "vulva" or, in a word borrowed from Sanskrit, the "yoni" (which means both "vulva" and "womb"). The term "vagina" does not mean the same thing. The vagina is the tube-like structure leading from the vulva to the cervix of the uterus, It is an internal structure that is not visible from the outside of the body.

The vulva is comprised of many anatomical sub-structures, and is much more complex than most people realize. The most visible external structures are the mons pubis or pubic mound, the pudendal cleft (the furrow at the base of the mons pubis where it divides to form the labia majora), and the labia majora. Behind them are perineum and the anus. In some women, the labia minora are also externally visible. (See Figure 13.)

When gently opened, the vulva reveals further anatomical structures: the labia minora, the glans of the clitoris, the prepuce or clitoral hood, and the structures of the vulvar vestibule, including the urethral orifice and the introitus or entrance to the vagina. (See Figure 14.)

THE LABIA MAJORA

The labia majora ("large lips" in Latin) are two folds of skin; in some women they are more like mounds than folds. They define the pudendal cleft, and conceal and protect the more delicate structures of the vulva.

The size and shape of the labia majora vary considerably. The labia majora of young girls are usually flat and smooth, having the same colour as the surrounding tissue. With the onset of puberty, and increase in body fat, the labia majora become more prominent. The front portion is usually thicker than the rear, tapering down and merging with the perineum.

In adulthood, the outer surfaces of the labia majora may have a different colour than the surrounding tissue. They may appear smooth or wrinkled, with a surface appearance like the scrotum, their male counterpart.

With increasing age, smooth labia majora may lose some of their fat content, becoming flatter and more wrinkled in appearance. After the onset of puberty the outer surfaces are usually covered with hair. When a woman is sexually aroused, the labia majora may darken or become reddish in colour, as blood flow increases in the area.

The inner surfaces are smooth and shiny, and the skin colour is dependent on a person's skin tone, varying from light pink to dark brown.

The visible structures when the labia majora are spread are the labia minora, prepuce, clitoral glans, frenum, vestibule, urethral meatus, vaginal introitus or hymen (depending on its presence or absence), fossa, and posterior fourchette.

THE LABIA MINORA

Although the name labia minora literally means "minor lips" in Latin, a significant percentage of women have labia minora that are large and prominent. Projecting out between the labia majora, they may not be totally concealed and thus are always visible. Other names for them are vaginal lips or nymphæ. The latter is the plural of nympha ("a nymph").

Every vulva is different, and to the vulvamancer, the most obvious differences among the vulvas of various women will be seen when comparing the size and shape of their nymphæ. Not only are they variable in symmetry, length, size, and shape, they change over time and are known to permanently darken in colour after pregnancy.

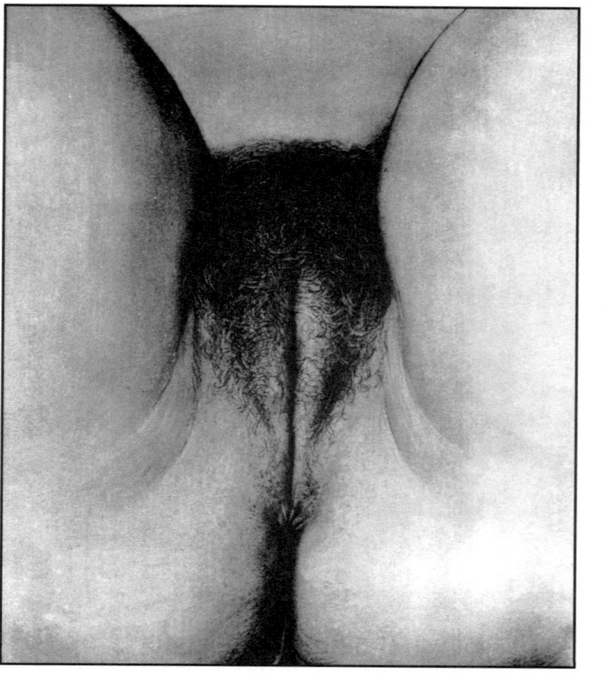

Fig. 13. Female vulva, external view; the labia majora hide the labia minora; art by R. L. Dickinson. See page 18.

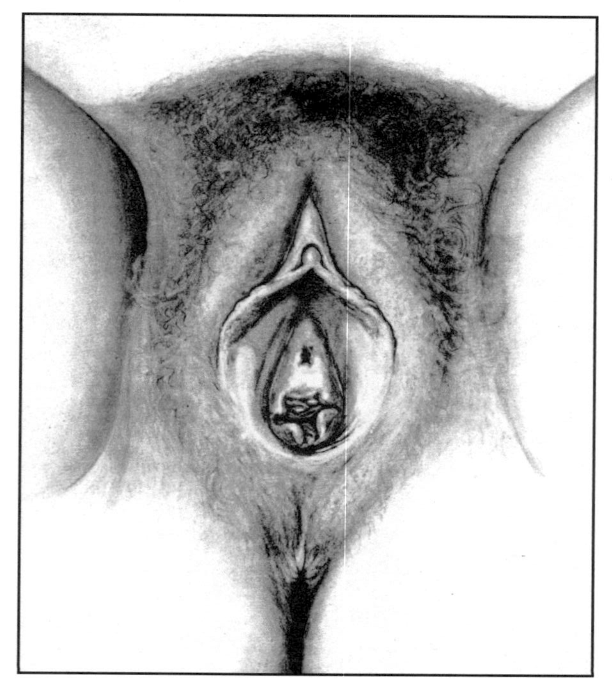

Fig. 14. Female vulva, spread open to reveal the labia minora et al; art by R. L. Dickinson. See page 18.

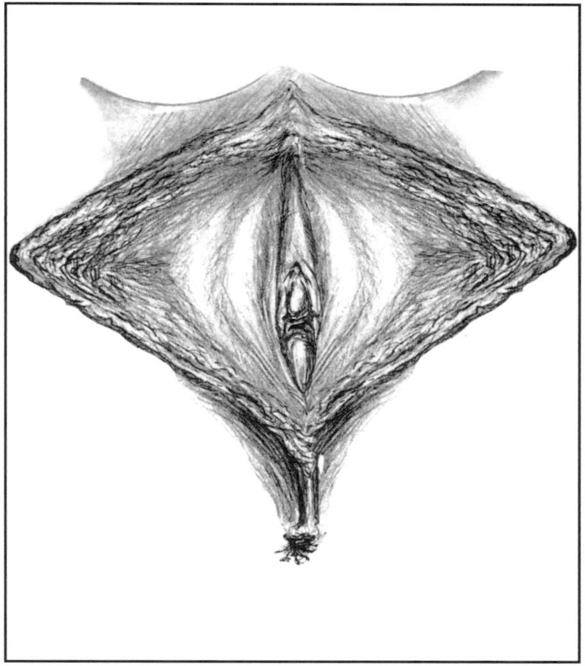

Fig. 15. Distended labia minora; naturally long or elongated by pulling; art by R. L. Dickinson. See page 18.

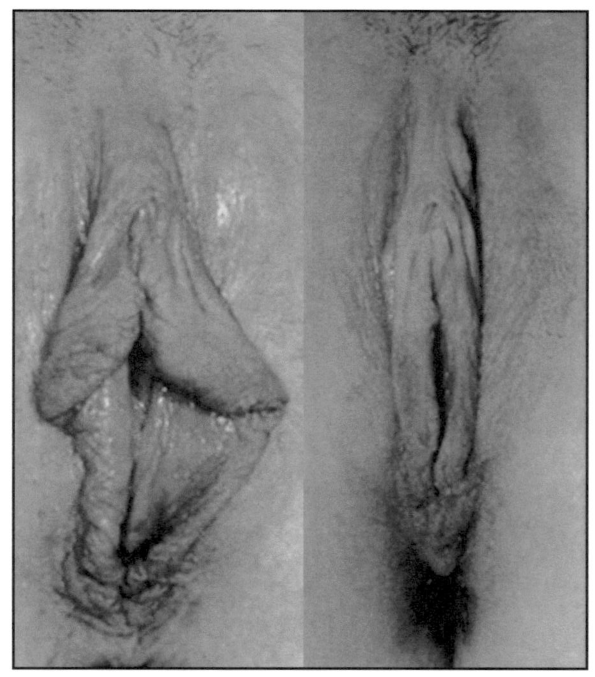

Fig. 16. Pre and post reduction labiaplasty; the labia minora have been cut off like a dog's ears. See page 28.

THE CLITORIS

The clitoris is a specialized organ with only one known function, to give women sexual pleasure. The small rounded structure that can be seen as a little "button" at the upper end of the vulva is the glans or tip of the clitoris. The clitoris itself is a much larger, bifurcated or Y-shaped structure with a large internal component that actually surrounds the vagina.

While the glans of the clitoris are usually small in size, it becomes engorged during sexual excitement and enlarges, much as the glans of the male penis does. The glans can contain as many as 8,000 nerve endings.

There is much variation in clitoral glans size from woman to woman and, depending upon hormone levels, they can grow quite large. Some can be just as large as a small penis, but they generally range from 1 - 15 mm. (0.04 - 0.6 inches, a little more than half an inch) in diameter. The average size of the non-erect glans is 4 - 5 mm. (0.15 - 0.2 inches, a little less than a quarter inch) in diameter,

The structure of the clitoris was first described in 1559 by the anatomist Realdo Colombo. This was almost 50 years after the first scientific anatomic drawings of "The Female Sexual Organs" were made by Leonardo da Vinci, circa 1510. Current scientists and art historians theorize that Leonardo's striking lack of understanding of female anatomy was due to a lack of interest in female genitalia because he was homosexual. That the clitoris went ignored for a half century is hardly shocking to most women of today.

In 1949, the anatomist Robert Latou Dickinson published detailed dissection drawings of the entire clitoris, including the glans, the upward shaft of the clitoris, its downward bend at the "clitoral knee," its branching into two "legs" (the crura), and its "embrace"of the penis during intercourse.

In 1999, the Australian researcher Helen O'Connell made a media splash when she claimed that the clitoris, considered in its entirety, may be larger than the penis.

In 2009, the French researchers Dr. Odile Buisson and Dr. Pierre Foldès produced the first 3-D sonography of the stimulated clitoris, providing a fuller understanding of how the erectile tissue of the clitoris engorges and surrounds the vagina. Buisson and Foldès revealed how what was once considered to be a vaginal orgasm is actually an internal clitoral orgasm and demonstrated that the so-called erogenous G-spot might be explained as the point where the anterior vaginal wall contacts the internal clitoris.

THE CLITORAL PREPUCE OR HOOD

Like the male foreskin, the clitoral prepuce or "hood" is formed of two layers, the outer layer extending from the body of the clitoris, and the inner layer comprised of mucous membrane. The hood protects the clitoral glans from irritation. It usually conceals the clitoral glans unless it is manually retracted, but the glans of some women may be always partially or completely exposed, and in some women the hood is absent.

The labia minora merge with the prepucc and attach to the base of the glans at a point called the frenum or frenulum. Because of this attachment, when the inner labia move as the penis enters and withdraws from the vagina during coitus, the clitoris is indirectly stimulated. Although the labia minora merge with the prepuce, they are comprised of structurally different tissues, a difference more obvious in some women than others.

THE VESTIBULE AND HART'S LINE

The vestibule is a triangle-shaped area below the clitoris and above the fourchette, with the labia minora defining the sides. The sides of the vestibule are visible as a distinct line on the inside of the inner lips. This line, which marks the change from the outer vulvar skin to the smoother skin of the inner vulva, is called "Hart's Line."

THE INTROITUS

The vaginal orifice or introitus is located within the vestibule. It forms the mouth of the vagina. Many people wrongly call it the "vaginal opening" but unless something is inserted into the vagina, the vaginal passage is closed and its walls are in contact with one another. The vagina is not a "hole." Rather it is a potential space.

THE URETHRAL MEATUS

The urethral meatus is the opening into the urethra, through which urine passes from the bladder. The size and shape of the urethral opening varies considerably from one woman to the next, as does its position, high or low, with respect to the introitus.

THE HYMEN

The thin membrane that conceals the vaginal canal is called the hymen. Depending on the force applied when objects are inserted into the vagina, it will either stretch or tear. Using tampons should not have any significant effect on the hymen, but the appearance of the introitus is likely to change when a woman inserts fingers or other objects into her vagina, and it is often partially torn during a woman's first sexual intercourse. Over time, as the hymen is repeatedly stretched open, it may slowly diminish, but it typically does not disappear altogether until a woman delivers a baby vaginally.

THE FOURCHETTE, THE PERINEUM, AND THE FOSSA

The posterior fourchette is the area where the labia minora join together below the vaginal introitus. It is the forward edge of the perineum, which is the space between the vulva and the anus. The fossa is the depression between the perineum and hymen, below the vaginal opening.

THE ANUS

The anus, which opens into the rectum, marks the posterior border of the perineum. Although not part of the vulva, the anus and rectum may be considered as erogenous zones by some women.

CHANGES TO THE VULVA OVER TIME

Over the course of a woman's lifetime, her genitals will change in appearance more than once. The events most likely to affect the overall appearance of the vulva are puberty, sexual intercourse, pregnancy, vaginal childbirth, and menopause.

In particular, during delivery, the perineum may tear or a doctor may make an incision, called an episiotomy. In either case, the resulting scar tissue will be visible. Later, during menopause, as the level of female hormones decreases, all tissues which are sensitive to these hormones will diminish in size, and become less elastic and moist

The appearance of the vulva can also change on a moment to moment basis, reflecting excitement, boredom, satisfaction, health, and happiness.

THE EROGENOUS ZONES OF THE FEMALE GENITALIA

The Clitoris

The clitoris is a specific anatomic structure whose only function is as a pleasure-giving erogenous zone. Remember that the clitoris is more than the visible glans, for the crura (forks or legs) are also part of the structure. A great deal of the pleasure a woman experiences during sexual contact comes from stimulation of the clitoral glans, but for many women, that pleasure is heightened if the two internal crura are further stimulated by the pressure of enclosing a penis or something firm of a similar shape.

The Gräfenberg Spot

The G-spot, also called the Gräfenberg spot, is an erogenous area of the vagina that, when stimulated, is said to lead to strong sexual arousal, powerful orgasms, and female ejaculation. It is said to be located 1-3 inches (2.5-7.6 cm) from the introitus on the anterior vaginal wall. Some describe this area as spongy with a rougher texture than other areas of the vaginal walls. As noted previously, it has been suggested that the G-spot might be the point where the anterior vaginal wall contacts the internal clitoris. Many women report, however, that they feel nothing special about this spot.

The Anterior Fornix Erogenous Zone

The anterior fornix erogenous zone, also known as the AFE or A-spot is said to be located at the deepest point on the anterior wall of the vagina, at the entrance to the anterior fornix, above the cervix, where it starts to curve upward. Stimulating the AFE zone reportedly leads to rapid vaginal lubrication and arousal, and intense orgasms without any other form of additional stimulation. Again, many women are not sexually pleased by contact with this spot and prefer stimulation of the "good old clitoris."

The Anus

The clitoris is shaped like a wishbone whose branches extend all the way down to the anus, and it indirectly receives stimulation during anal penetration. In addition, an anally-stimulated orgasm may occur through indirect stimulation of the G-spot. Men are generally more able to achieve climax through anal sex because of the location of the male prostate, which is an erogenous zone unto itself.

GENITAL MODIFICATION AND MUTILATION

Not only do yonis congenitally differ in appearance, shape, and size, they can be modified through surgical and non-surgical means. Familiarity with these practices and their outcomes is essential to the yoni reader.

- **Cosmetic Genital Modification:** This refers to elective procedures undertaken voluntarily by a mentally and legally competent adult woman acting on her own behalf. Such genital modifications can be permanent or temporary, and they can logically be compared to other forms of permanent or temporary body modification, such as adult circumcision, cosmetic plastic surgery, tattooing, and piercing.
- **Medical Genital Modification:** This refers to surgical interventions that alter the female genitalia for medical reasons. Such interventions, generally undertaken by a doctor, may be performed with or without the patient's fully informed consent as to the visual outcome. The most common of these procedures is the episiotomy. Non-consensual modification of the genitalia of intersex children is also practiced.
- **Genital Mutilation:** This refers to invasive surgical procedures intended to permanently disfigure the natural genitalia or to reduce or eliminate genital functionality. In some cases these mutilations can be remediated with plastic surgery; in other cases, such as clitorectomy, the removal of tissue renders them irreversible.

COSMETIC GENITAL MODIFICATION

Labia Stretching and Elongation

Labia stretching, medically known as sinus pudoris or macronympha, is the act of elongating the labia minora by repeated manual pulling or by use of physical equipment such as weights. In Rwanda, Uganda, Burundi, Malawi, and other Sub-Saharan African countries, it is a familiar cultural practice. It is also undertaken as a form of body modification elsewhere.

Reasons to engage in labia stretching include sexual enhancement, æsthetics, symmetry (women with unequally long labia may increase the size of the shorter to achieve evenness), and personal gratification. In several African nations, elongated labia are said to facilitate orgasm and female ejaculation, and to enhance sexual pleasure for both partners. (See Figure 15.)

Although labial elongation has been compared to genital mutilation, there are marked differences. Female genital cutting is intended to reduce a girl's sexual desire, while labial elongation is an attempt to enhance it. The World Health Organization previously identified labial stretching as a form of "mutilation," but it does not violate women's rights, in that it does not involve physical violence, unless the woman is misled as to its benefits or is a child under the legal age of consent.

In Rwanda, female family members teach girls at puberty how to pull their labia to lengthen them. Women continue the practice, which is called guguna imishino ("labia pulling"), into adulthood. The most important aspect of this act is to assist the woman to ejaculate when a man strokes the elongated labia gently without any form of sexual penetration.

In Zimbabwe and Uganda the amount of labial elongation varies from woman to woman, but there is a general view that the inner labia benefit from being longer than they would be naturally. Women in these countries have reported that elongated inner labia swell more during sexual excitement, and in doing so, provide a bigger surface area for penile friction during coitus. They also swell inwards, partially blocking the entrance to the vagina. The process of elongating the labia is part of the transformation from a girl to a woman, a rite of passage much like ear piercing or tattooing among teenaged girls in America.

Labia elongation is also practiced among the Khoisan people of southern Africa, resulting in the inner labia often being several centimeters longer than the outer labia. The stretching is usually done by an aunt on girls beginning at the age of four or five, a practice bordering on female genital mutilation, because the children are below the age of consent, although this designation is contested by some practitioners.

Europeans called the Khoisans "Hottentots," and in the 18th century they coined the term "hottentot apron" to describe the elongated labia found among women from this region The word "apron" came about because early European descriptions misidentified the pair of labia as a single organ, which they called an "apron." The seemingly neutral term "hottentot apron" conceals the disdain with which this cosmetic feature was viewed by Europeans, and especially by doctors who claimed that "hypertrophic labia" indicated moral deviance, a high sexual appetite, and racial inferiority.

In modern times labia elongation is seen as a cosmetic choice, and women born outside of Sub-Saharan Africa may practice it for personal gratification in the same way that they might undertake stretched earlobe piercings.

Labiaplasty

Labiaplasty is the term used to describe reparative or cosmetic surgery of the labia majora or minora. It is used to restore injured labia, to reduce the size of long labia, or to enlarge labia that have diminished due to aging.

The flaccid labia majora and labia minora of adult women vary in length from less than an inch to more than 4 inches, and a very wide-spread pair of labia minora can reach 8 1/2 inches tip-to-tip. These variations are primarily a matter of genetics and are not caused by intentional manual stretching, "excessive masturbation" (whatever that is!), or child sexual abuse.

Women with asymmetrical labia minora may seek to "even up" their mismatched nymphæ through reduction labiaplasty, but the procedure is also on the rise in a more radical form that amounts to labia removal. The newfound urban cultural desire for tiny labia minora is controversial, and "intactivist" critics of the procedure warn that, as with male circumcision, amputation of the nerve-rich tissues can lead to loss of sexual sensation. (See Figure 16).

Augmentation labiaplasty is undertaken to increase the fullness of labia majora that have diminished due to post-menopausal aging or extreme weight loss. Involuted outer labia can also be corrected by this method. Augmentation labiaplasty is accomplished by injecting fat taken from another part of the woman's body. It is generally offered by cosmetic surgeons who also perform facelifts, breast augmentation, botox and filler injections, and liposuction. Insofar as augmentation labiaplasty is restorative of a woman's youthful appearance, it is less controversial than reduction labiaplasty.

The rise in labiaplasty, both for reduction and augmentation, has produced a backlash in the so-called "labia pride movement." The major point of contention is that heavy advertising for these cosmetic labial procedures, in combination with a lack of public education, fosters body insecurities in women, in spite of the fact that there is wide variation in the size of labia between women as well as in the individual woman over the course of her life.

Clitoral Hood Reduction

Clitoral hood reduction, also termed clitoral hoodectomy, clitoral unhooding, clitoridotomy, or partial hoodectomy, is an elective procedure for reducing the size of the clitoral prepuce in order to more fully expose the glans of the clitoris. As with male circumcision, there may be a stated therapeutic goal to improve sexual functioning, but this surgery is usually undertaken in the belief that it enhances the æsthetic refinement of the vulva.

Elective Hymenoplasty

Hymenoplasty is the surgical modification of the hymen. The term comes from the Greek word hymen meaning "membrane." Generally, there are two types of hymemoplasty surgeries: hymenotomy and hymenorrhaphy.

Hymenotomy is the surgical removal of the hymen. It is performed on women whose hymens are imperforate and do not permit the flow of menses, and on those with microperforate or septate hymens comprised of sieve-like or banded tissue structures that will not permit vaginal intercourse.

Hymenorrhaphy or hymen reconstruction surgery entails restoration of the hymen. It is available from some plastic surgery centers, generally as day surgery. The aim is to cause bleeding during post-nuptial intercourse, which in some cultures is considered proof of pre-marital virginity. Certain hymen reconstruction operations are legal in some countries, while other countries ban all forms of hymenorrhaphy.

In the purely cosmetic form of hymenorrhaphy, a membrane without blood supply is created in the area of the hymen, sometimes including a gelatin capsule containing an artificial blood-like substance. This operation is intended to be performed within a few days before an intended marriage. Another form of the procedure utilizes a flap of the vaginal lining, complete with its blood supply, to create a new hymen. Patients are advised to refrain from penetrative sex for up to three months following this procedure.

Non-Surgical Hymenoplasty

An intact or "virgin" hymen is so important in some cultures that "do it yourself at home" non-surgical hymen restoration kits are being sold on the internet. For example, one online company advertises that its product uses medical grade red liquid dye in a translucent membrane to give a similar effect to real human blood. The kit contains a sealed package containing an artificial hymen. This is carefully placed inside the vagina 15 - 20 minutes prior to intercourse. The purchaser is instructed to "Insert the Artificial Hymen into your vagina carefully. It will expand a little and make you feel tight. When your lover penetrates, it will ooze out a liquid that appears like blood, not too much but just the right amount. Add in a few moans and groans and you will pass through undetectable! It's easy to use, clinically proven non-toxic to humans and has no side effects, no pain to use, and no allergic reaction."

Cosmetic Genital Piercing

Genital piercings have become fairly common in the 21st century and there are numerous types:

- **Labia Majora and Labia Minora Piercing:** Sometimes, for the purposes of BDSM chastity play, labial piercings include closure with a padlock through both of the labia minora.
- **The Clitoral Glans Piercing:** This structure is small in many women, hence this piercing is not very common.
- **The Clitoral Hood Piercing:** This is the most common genital piercing. It can be applied horizontally or vertically.
- **The Deep Hood Piercing:** This is a variation of the clitoral hood piercing that passes deeper through the clitoral hood.
- **The Isabella Piercing:** This passes vertically through the clitoral shaft, an area that is rather difficult to pierce.
- **The Triangle Piercing:** This is located at the ventral end of the labia minora, at the point of transition between labia and clitoral hood. It runs horizontally, partly under the clitoral shaft.
- **The Fourchette Piercing:** This passes through the dorsal rim of the vulval vestibule.
- **The Suitcase Piercing:** A version of the Fourchette, the Suitcase can be considered as a deep Fourchette; it enters on the perineum.
- **The Princess Albertina Piercing:** The female version of the Prince Albert piercing, this passes through the dorsal wall of the urethra.
- **The Christina Piercing:** This is a surface piercing, situated on the lower part of the mons pubis.
- **The Nefertiti Piercing:** This is a combination between the Christina piercing and the vertical clitoral hood piercing.
- **The Guiche Piercing:** This is not truly a genital piercing, as it passes horizontally through the perineum.
- **The Anal Piercing:** This passes through the anus and, as such, it is not a true genital piercing, but it may be combined with one.

Many of these piercings can be pleasurable to the woman wearing them because there is extra stimulation applied to the genitals. Needless to say, cleanliness and good aftercare are essential to health when undertaking genital and anal piercings.

Tattooing and Other Decorations

The tattooing of female genitals has become increasingly popular in the 21st century, and a vulvar tattoo is colloquially known as "vatoo" or a "twatoo." The vatoo is a permanent decoration, and may be combined with pubic hair removal to enhance its visibility.

The colloquial term "vajazzling" is used to describe short-term, non-permanent peri-vulvar decorations such as the application of make-up, glitter, temporary tattoos, and other external decorations.

Vulvar Colouring

There are two types of colour modifications: vulvar skin lightening, whitening, or bleaching and vulvar skin dyeing.

Commercial skin lightening products, such as Clean & Dry Intimate Wash have been marketed to women, particularly in India, to render the skin of the vulva more pale. They have caused great controversy because of the link between skin colour and social hierarchy in India.

My New Pink Button is typical of the temporary vulvar dyes. It is advertised as a product meant to "restore the youthful pink colour back to your labia." The company claims to have been founded by a "female certified Paramedical Æsthetician after she discovered her own genital colour loss." Apparently, "while looking online for a solution, she discovered thousands of other women asking the same questions regarding their colour loss. After countless searches revealing no solution available and a discussion with her own gynecologist, she decided to create her own." The product has several different shades from which to choose and each kit includes 20 disposable applicators, mixing dish, labia colourant dye and instructional guide.

G-Spot Amplification

G-spot amplification (also called G-spot augmentation or, colloquially, the "G-Shot") is not strictly cosmetic (it cannot be seen) but although it is performed by a gynecological surgeon, it is an elective procedure with no basis in medical necessity. The goal is to temporarily increase pleasure in sexually active women with normal sexual function by increasing the size and sensitivity of the G-spot. The doctor attempts to locate the G-spot and notes measurements for future reference. After numbing the area with a local anesthetic, human engineered collagen is then injected directly under the mucosa in the area self-identified by the patient as the location of her G-spot.

MEDICAL GENITAL MODIFICATION

Medical Hymenotomy or Opening the Hymen

A hymenotomy is a minor medical procedure involving the surgical removal or opening of the hymen. It is often performed on patients with imperforate hymens or septate hymens, or other situations where the hymen is unusually thick or rigid. In the case of a female with a hymen without any opening, an opening may be created in order to facilitate menstruation. In situations where the opening is extremely small or the band(s) of a septate hymen limit access to the vaginal opening, the individual may elect for hymenotomy to allow for comfortable sexual penetration of her vagina, or to relieve pain or discomfort when inserting or removing tampons.

Medical Hymenorrhaphy or Hymen Reconstruction

Suturing of a tear in the hymen caused by sexual assault may be performed soon after the assault in order to facilitate healing. In France, some of the cost is reimbursed by the state in cases of rape or trauma.

Episiotomy

An episiotomy (also known by the less-widely used term perineotomy) is a surgical incision on the perineum and the posterior vaginal wall. The incision is commonly performed under local anesthetic (pudendal anesthesia) during childbirth, and is sutured close after delivery. It is one of the most common medical procedures performed on women. However, its routine use in childbirth has steadily declined in recent decades.

For several generations doctors thought a "clean cut" would be better than a "messy tear." The cut was supposed to help women heal more easily, experience less urinary incontinence, and enjoy a better sex life.

In 2005, a large study found that episiotomies not only didn't improve recovery times or pain after birth but increased the risk of deeper tears and pelvic floor problems. While most first time moms do tear during childbirth, most tears are superficial 1st, or 2nd degree tears, affecting only the surface of the body. Occasionally women tear into the muscle but an episiotomy always cuts through the muscle and can lead to deeper 3rd or 4th degree tears, kind of like when you snip the edge of a piece of cloth, which can make it rip more easily.

In 2006 the American College of Obstetrics and Gynecology changed their guidelines, discouraging episiotomies unless medically necessary.

"Medically necessary" typically means that the baby needs to be vaginally delivered immediately and there isn't time to wait for the perineum to stretch slowly. In this scenario, an episiotomy has fewer risks compared to a c-section. However, a landmark 2005 study on home births published in the *British Medical Journal* tracked over 5,000 mothers in the US and Canada, and found the episiotomy rate was 2.1% at home births versus 33% in hospital births. The very different rates of episiotomy for these low-risk births suggest that care-provider preference and context play a key role in the determination of "medical necessity." Nonetheless, with each new generation of Ob/GYNs, the episiotomy rates, even in hospitals, continue to decline.

There are four main types of episiotomy and each produces its own distinct scar. The yoni reader should be aware of all of them:

- **Mediolateral:** The incision is made downward and outward from midpoint of the fourchette either to right or left. It is directed diagonally in a straight line which runs about 2.5 cm away from the anus (midpoint between anus and ischial tuberosity or "stting bone").
- **Median:** The incision commences from the center of the fourchette and extends on the posterior side along the midline for 2.5 cm.
- **Lateral:** The incision starts from about 1 cm away from the center of the fourchette and extends laterally. Drawbacks to this form of incision include the chance of injury to Bartholin's duct; thus some practitioners have totally condemned it.
- **J-Shaped:** The incision begins in the center of the fourchette and is directed posteriorly along the midline for about 1.5 cm and then directed downwards and outwards along a 5 or 7 o'clock position to avoid the anal sphincter. This is also not done widely.

There are stories told of the "husband's knot," "lover's knot," or "happy husband's stitch" – an extra stitch taken when repairing the cut after an episiotomy to create a tighter vaginal opening. While this procedure may have been performed in the past, it is not currently common, because generally accepted surgical practice is to approximate the tissues exactly as they were naturally, prior to the episiotomy.

FEMALE GENITAL MUTILATION

The World Health Organization defines female genital mutilation as the "partial or total removal of the external female genitalia or other injury to the female genital organs for non-medical reasons" and identifies four categories:

- **Type I, Clitoridectomy:** Partial or total removal of the clitoris and/or the prepuce
  - **Type Ia:** Removal of the clitoral hood or prepuce only
  - **Type Ib:** Removal of the clitoris with the prepuce
- **Type II, Excision:** Partial or total removal of the clitoris and the labia minora, with or without excision of the labia majora
  - **Type IIa:** Removal of the labia minora only
  - **Type IIb:** Partial or total removal of the clitoris and labia minora
  - **Type IIc:** Partial or total removal of the clitoris, the labia minora and the labia majora
- **Type III, Infibulation:** Narrowing of the vaginal orifice with creation of a covering seal by cutting and appositioning the labia minora and/or the labia majora, with or without excision of the clitoris
  - **Type IIIa:** Removal and apposition of the labia minora
  - **Type IIIb:** Removal and apposition of the labia majora
- **Type IV, Other Harmful Procedures**: All other mutilations of the female genitalia for non-medical purposes, such as pricking, piercing, incising, scraping and cauterization

Ritual Female Genital Mutilation

Ritualized female genital mutilation is practiced in 27 countries in Sub-Saharan and Northeast Africa, and to a lesser extent in Asia, the Middle East, and within immigrant communities elsewhere. Rooted in gender inequality; ideas about purity, modesty, and æsthetics; and attempts to control women's sexuality, it is supported by both women and men, who see it as a source of honour and authority, and an essential part of raising a daughter well. Techniques vary, but typically the mutilation is performed with a knife or razor, with or without anesthesia, on girls whose age varies from weeks after birth to puberty. In half the countries for which figures were available in 2013, most girls were mutilated before the age of five. In some nations the ritual practice has been outlawed, but still persists, due to cultural beliefs.

Pseudo-Medical Female Genital Mutilation

Vaginal cutting, also known as gishiri or ghishri cutting, is performed by the Hausa and Fulani people of Northern Nigeria and Southern Niger, where it is prescribed by traditional healers to treat a variety of gynecological ailments, although there is no scientific basis for this belief.

Medical gynecologists in 19th-century Europe and the United States removed the external clitoris for various pseudo-medical reasons.

The first reported clitoridectomy in Europe was carried out in 1822 by Karl Ferdinand von Græfe (1787-1840), a surgeon in Berlin, on a teenage girl, regarded as an "imbecile," who was masturbating.

Isaac Baker Brown (1812–1873), an English gynecologist, president of the Medical Society of London, and co-founder of St. Mary's Hospital in London, believed that "unnatural irritation" of the clitoris caused epilepsy, hysteria, and mania, and "set to work to remove [it] whenever he had the opportunity of doing so," according to his obituary in the *Medical Times and Gazette*. When he published his views in a book, *On the Curability of Certain Forms of Insanity, Epilepsy, Catalepsy, and Hysteria in Females* (1866), he was accused of quackery, mutilation, and operating without consent. Expelled from the Obstetrical Society, he died in poverty.

J. Marion Sims (1813-1883) is regarded as the father of gynecology in the United States — controversially so because of his experimental surgery on slaves. In 1862 he slit the neck of a woman's uterus and amputated her clitoris, "for the relief of the nervous or hysterical condition as recommended by Baker Brown," after she complained of period pain, convulsions, and bladder problems.

Sources differ as to when the last clitoridectomy was performed in the United States. G. J. Barker-Benfield writes that the practice continued until at least 1904 and perhaps into the 1920s. A 1985 paper in the *Obstetrical and Gynecological Survey* said it was performed into the 1960s to treat "hysteria, erotomania, and lesbianism."

The Human Toll of Female Genital Mutilation

Removal of the external clitoris may leave a woman incapable of orgasm. Infibulation in which a small hole is left for the passage of urine and menstrual blood, and the wound is opened up for intercourse and childbirth, may lead to painful intercourse. Other side-effects include recurrent infections, chronic pain, cysts, infertility, complications during childbirth, and fatal bleeding.

THE ORIGINS OF YONI READING

THE ANANGA RANGA

The classification of the yoni into four basic types was first described in an Indian sex manual written by Kalyana Malla in the 15th or 16th century. Titled the *Ananga Ranga (Stage of Love)* or *Kamaledhiplava (Boat in the Sea of Love)*, it was written in honour of Lad Khan, son of Ahmed Khan Lodi. This work is often compared to the *Kama Sutra*, upon which it draws. Chapter one explains the four orders of women and their respective yonis. They are known as Padmini, Chatrini, Shankhini, and Hastini.

- **Padmini:** Also known as the "lotus woman," the Padmini is described as having a yoni that resembles the open lotus bud; she only sleeps a small amount, is respectable, and religious. She possesses the walk of a Swan. Her face is pleasing as the full moon. Her body, well clothed with flesh, is as soft as the (tall fragrant tree known as) the Shiras or Mustard flower. Her yoni resembles the opening Lotus bud and her kama-salila (vaginal lubrication) is perfumed like the "Lilly, which has newly burst." She enjoys feeling the rays of the sun, that is, to be seen in daylight, and the strong touch of hands.
- **Chitrini:** Also known as the "art woman" or "fancy woman," she has a medium sized body and a walk like that of an elephant. She loves to sing and she loves pets. She is a middle-sized woman, neither short nor tall, with bee-black hair and a thin, round, shell-like neck. She has a tender body. Her waist is lean-girthed as the Lion's. She has hard, full breasts and heavy hips. The hair is thin about her yoni. The mons veneris or pubic mound is soft, raised and round. Her kama-salila is exceptionally hot and abundant, smells sweet, and tastes like honey.
- **Shankhini:** Also known as the "conch woman" or "fairy woman," she is described as having a temperament that is sometimes hot-headed and confused; she is also described as having a body that is large with small breasts and a yoni that is moist. She is of bilious temperament, her skin being always hot and tawny or dark yellow-brown. Her body is large, her waist thick and her breasts small. Her yoni is ever moist with kama-salila, which is distinctly salty and the cleft is covered with thick hair. Her yoni loves to be kissed and licked.

- **Hastini:** Also known as the "Elephant woman," the Hastini is short, has light skin, large hips, and a harsh voice. She can only be truly satisfied by prolonged sex. Her yoni is large and deep, and enjoys much stimulation of the clitoris. She is short in stature. She has a stout, course body and her skin, if fair, is dead white. Her hair is tawny, her lips are large, her voice is harsh, choked and throaty. Her neck is bent. Her kama-salila has the savour of the juice which flows in the Spring from the musky perspiration that collects on a rutting Elephant's forehead.

In Chapter One, and also in section three of the *Ananga Ranga* there is a table which classifies the greatest days of enjoyment for the four classes of women. In section four certain hours are prescribed for highest enjoyment.

In Chapter Two, Malla describes "The Various Seats of Passion in Women." The four classes of women have different ways to enjoy their sexual desires and achieve satisfaction. The husband is advised to continue his action until he sees the body-hair bristle and hears the sitkara (an inarticulate sound of climax produced by drawing in the air between the closed teeth); then he will know that his wife is truly satisfied. In this chapter Malla also gives four tables of manipulation (ways of pleasuring one's wife), each related to one of the four classes of women:

- **Padmini:** Manipulate her throat, cheek, hair, waist, breast, back, bosom, side, thigh, belly, arm, lip, nipple, space between her eyes, and her foot.
- **Chitrini:** Manipulate her yoni, lower lip, throat, waist, navel, lip, breast, ear, thigh, back, butt, forehead, chest, hair, eye, and middle-body.
- **Shankhini:** Manipulate her body in general, lower lip, arm, breasts, belly, chest, throat, ear, foot, mouth, face, yoni, lip, inch below her head, and the lower edge of her yoni.
- **Hastini:** Manipulate her yoni, navel, lip, side, breast, chest, nipple, body generally, eye, and armpit.

In Chapter Three, section two, the women are further subdivided into three categories; this is dependent upon the depth and extent of their yoni:

- **Mrigi (Harini)**: A Deer woman whose yoni is six fingers deep.
- **Vadava (Ashvini):** A Mare woman whose yoni is nine fingers deep.
- **Karini:** An Elephant woman whose yoni is twelve fingers in depth.

THE PERFUMED GARDEN

A complex and nuanced classification of yoni types was published in the 16th century Arabic erotic manual called Al-rawz al-ātir fī nuzhat al-hātir or *The Perfumed Garden,* as follows:

• **Abou Cheuffrine ("The Double-Lipped"):** A vulva with lips that are either long and hanging or exceptionally thick and large.

• **Abou Djebaha ("One With a Projection"):** A large vulva with a projecting, fleshy "forehead."

• **Abou Chochime ("The Snub-Nose"):** A vulva with thin lips and a small "tongue" or clitoris.

• **Abou Tertour ("The Crested One"):** A vulva with a red comb, like that of a Rooster, which rises at the moment of enjoyment.

• **El Addad ("The Biter"):** A synonym for El Deukkak; despite the name, it has no connection with the mythological vagina dentata (toothed vagina).

• **El Aride ("The Large One"):** The thick, fleshy vulva of a large woman.

• **El Ass ("The Primordial"):** A general term applied to any kind of vulva.

• **El Cheukk ("The Chink"):** The hard vulva of a very lean or bony woman "with not a vestige of flesh."

• **El Deukkak ("The Crusher"):** A vulva that makes crushing and clinging movements upon the penis once it has entered, takes him into her grip with the pelvic muscles and would, if possible, even absorb a man's testicles.

• **El Feurdj ("Passage, Opening, Slit"):** A generic Arabic term for the vulva. The same word is also applied to a pass between two mountains. With only tiny diacritical marks added, it means "deliverance from misfortunes."

• **El Gueunfond ("The Hedgehog"):** A vulva "dried up with age and with bristly hair."

• **El Hacene ("The Beautiful"):** A firm, plump vulva "without deformity," and "vaulted like a dome." Gazing at it makes a "feeble erection strong."

• **El Harr ("The Hot One"):** The "highly esteemed" vulva which is tight and warm, "possessing an intrinsic heat" that equals "the fire of love."

• **El Hezzaz ("The Restless"):** The eagerly moving vulva of a woman starved for sexual play and enjoyment. Very similar to the descriptions of El Moudd ("the accommodating") and El Mouaine ("the assistant").

• **El Harrab ("The Fugitive"):** A small, tight vulva that is also "short." Penetration is painful; she's a "fugitive" trying to evade contact with men.

• **El Keuss ("The Vulva"):** A "soft, seductive, perfect" and pleasantly smelling vulva of a young woman; plump and round "in every direction, with long lips, grand slit"; dry yet warm. The text follows this description with the prayer "May God grant us the possession of such a vulva! Amen."

• **El Laddid ("The Delicious"):** A vulva with "the reputation of affording unprecedented pleasure."

• **El Lezzaz ("The Unionist"):** A synonym for El Deukkak.

• **El Merour ("The Deep One"):** This one "always has the mouth open."

• **El Meusass ("The Sucker"):** A synonym for El Deukkak

• **El Meusbeul ("The Long One"):** A vulva reaching from pubis to anus. It lengthens when the woman is standing or lying down, yet contracts when she is sitting, "differing in this respect from the vulva of a round shape."

• **El Mokaour ("The Bottomless"):** A vulva leading to a deep vagina. Such a woman requires a specific partner or activity to arouse and satisfy her.

• **El Neuffakh ("The Swelling One"):** A vulva "opening and shutting convulsively," like "the vulva of a mare," at "the moment of climax."

• **El Ouasa ("The Vast One"):** A vulva that opens widely when excited.

• **El Relmoune ("The Voluptuous"):** The vulva of a young girl or woman before her first coitus (a so-called virgin).

• **El Sabeur ("The Resigned"):** The vulva of a woman who "suffers resignedly" any number of penetrations and even "violent and prolonged coition." Even after "a hundred times," and even with "several" partners, she would not be "annoyed" but would rather "give thanks to God."

• **El Sakouti ("The Silent One"):** The vulva of a woman who makes no noise, even if she is entered "a hundred times."

• **El Taleb ("The Yearning One"):** The vulva of a woman who has been abstinent for too long, or, who is more sexually demanding than her partner.

• **El Tseguil ("The Importunate"):** The tireless vulva of a free and passionate woman with strong sexual demands who "would want still more" even after "a hundred times." Typically fearful of such women who are the "pursuer" instead of the "pursued," the author writes: "Luckily, it is a rarity, and only found in a small number of women who are wild with passion, all on fire, aglow." Little did he know.

• **El Zerzour ("The Starling"):** The vulva of a very young girl.

• **El Zeunbour ("The Wasp"):** A vulva named for the nature of the pubic hair surrounding it, or, as the text says: "the strength and roughness of its fur." To the entering penis the hair feels like stings from a Wasp.

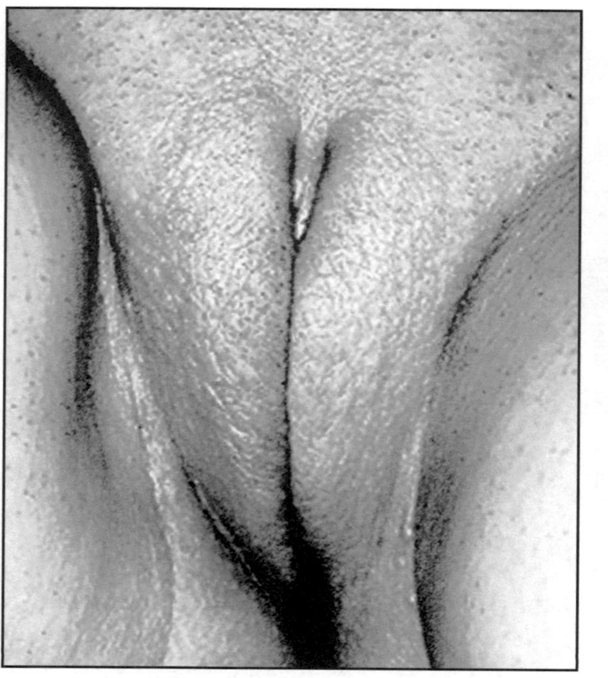

Fig. 17. Wider labia majora; the hair has been shaved to reveal th contours. See page 43.

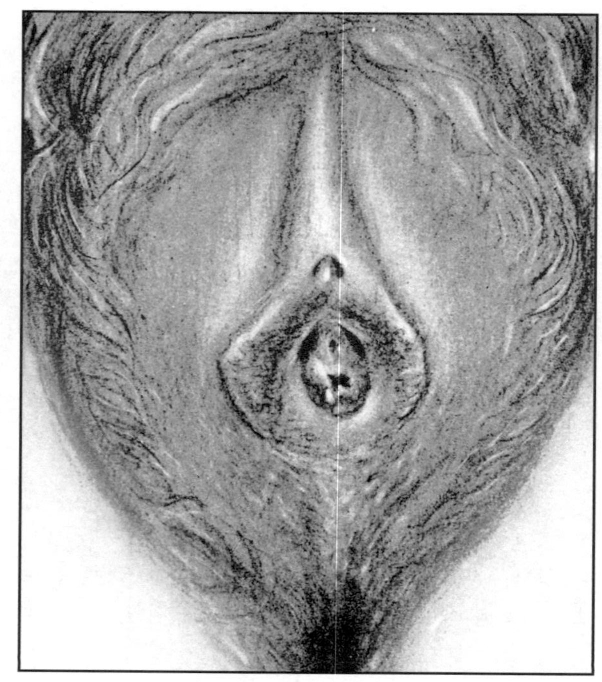

Fig. 18. Narrower labia majora; fairly flat and allowing exposure of the labia minora. See page 43.

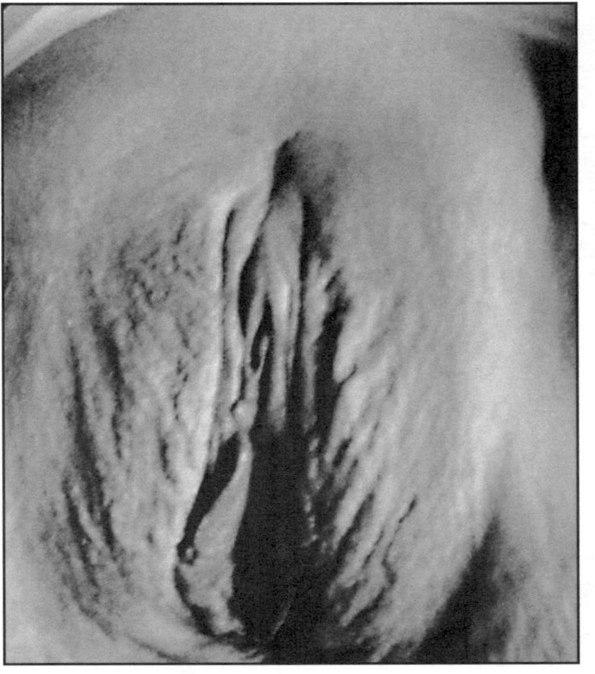

Fig. 19. Light labia majora; the hair has been shaved to reveal the features. See page 46.

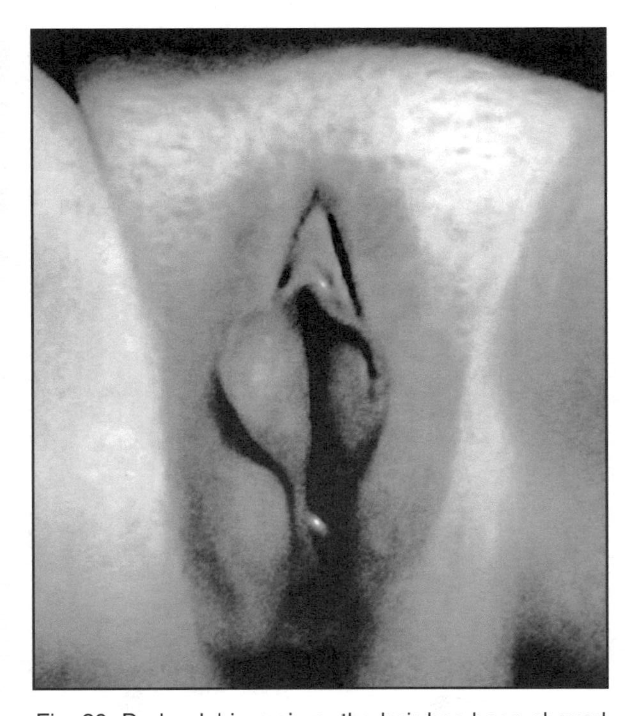

Fig. 20. Darker labia majora; the hair has been shaved to reveal the features. See page 46.

A COMPLETE YONI READING SYSTEM

As already noted, over the course of a woman's lifetime, her genitals will naturally (and perhaps artificially) change in appearance. The most dramatic natural changes occur with the large milestones: puberty, sex, pregnancy, post-pregnancy, and menopause. As with other anatomy-based reading systems like palmistry, breast analysis, and face reading, these life-cycle and age-related changes must be taken into consideration while reading.

However, unlike the hand, face, or breast, the appearance of the vulva also changes frequently without respect to age. Each month, circulating hormones have their changing effect. Superimposed on this natural cycle are the highs and lows of life and exposure to exogenous and endogenous hormones, generated by stress, happiness, etc. These hormones have their particular affects on the physiognomy of the vulva. For example, circulating steroids like cortisol increase in times of stress and chronic steroid exposure can lead to hypertrophy of the clitoral glans. Additionally, the vulva responds to the acute changes in personal feelings, excitement, boredom, contentment, etc., with changes in blood flow, colouring, and lubrication.

For the purposes of clarity and standardization, all terminology used is the modern, scientific, and accepted nomenclature, with reference to terms from previous eras and other cultures. This system draws in part upon older works, including the *Ananga Ranga*, *The Perfumed Garden*, the *Genital Horoscope* system of Martha Olschewski, and the private teachings of Julie Ann Johnson.

The vulvamancer is directed to perform the reading in the following steps.

1. **Pubic Mound and Pubic Hair**
2. **Labia Majora**
3. **Labia Minora**
4. **Prepuce or Clitoral Hood**
5. **Clitoral Glans**
6. **Scent**
7. **Discharge**
8. **Vaginal Lubrication or Kama-Salila**
9. **Female Ejaculate or Amrita**

Steps 1 through 6 are easily perceptible though sight, touch, and sense of smell; steps 7 through 9 require prolonged or intimate contact to assess.

STEP 1: READ THE PUBIC MOUND AND PUBIC HAIR

Since pubic hair is subject to grooming and hairstyles are subject to fashion trends, pubic hair patterns speak to a woman's conformity to norms.

Ancient Romans singed their pubic hair off. In some cultures it is plucked. At one time women wore pubic hair wigs or merkins to cover thinning pubic hair. Current fashions of waxing or shaving produce a sharply defined edge or remove all the hair. In 2016, a study by the University of California, San Francisco, established that pubic grooming abrades the skin and increases the risk of sexually transmitted herpes and human papillomavirus. The study also found that pubic groomers are more likely to engage in risky sexual behaviours with more sexual partners than non-groomers.

- **Vajazzled (tattooed, pierced, ornamented):** Boldly desires admiration, creative, a risk-taker, loves adventure, may place beauty above comfort.
- **Shaved or waxed:** Fashionable, wants to please, not afraid to be bold; wishes to appear child-like; may fear disease; may take risks.
- **Runway (narrow strip):** Keeps up with the times, wants to be wild, but not too wild; holds back sometimes; coy; has a sense of artistry.
- **Full, but neat, trimmed, or edged:** Wants to be well-groomed, but may not have the time for trends. Acknowledges the necessity of conformity.
- **Natural:** Bucks trends, respects nature, is anti-authoritarian. Fashion is not a priority. More interested in sex and sensuality than in appearance.

STEP 2: READ THE LABIA MAJORA

Prominence of the Labia Majora

As stated in the anatomy section, the labia majora become more prominent during puberty and may decrease in size in post-menopausal women.

- **Fleshy, wide:** A doer, active and busy, with quick reaction times; on an older woman, indicative of active, youthful ways. (See Figure 17.)
- **Thin, narrow, flat:** Has the wisdom that comes experience; on a young woman, an indication that she may have endured struggles, trials, and tribulations but ended up better for them. (See Figure 18.)
- **Blended type:** Fleshy and thin or wide yet flat labia majora indicate a blend of personality types or a woman who does not show her age.

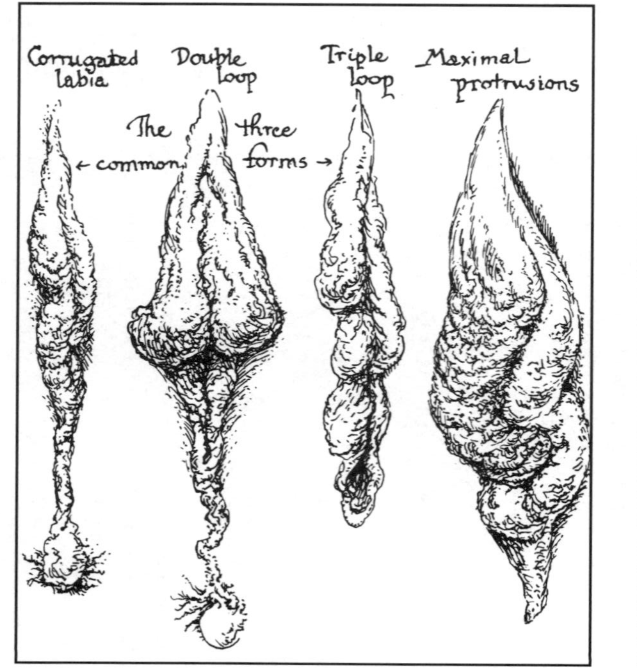

Fig. 21. Exposed labia minora; various forms drawn from life by Robert Latou Dickinson. See page 47.

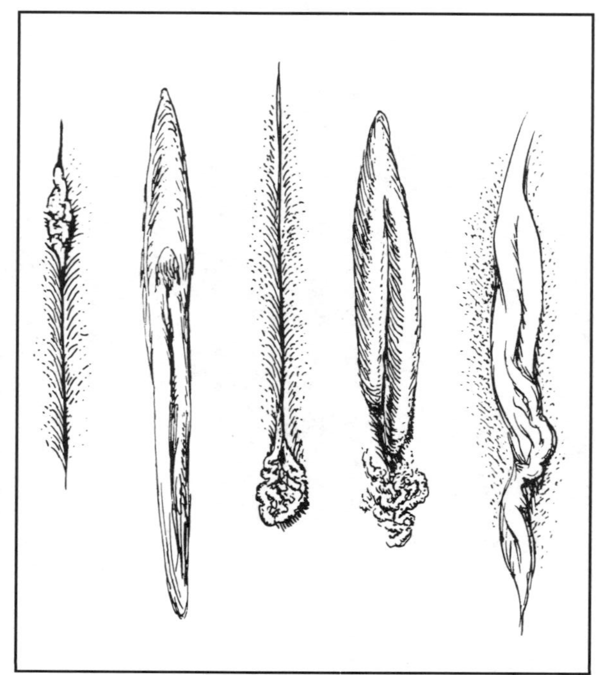

Fig. 22. Sheltered labia minora; various forms drawn from life by Robert Latou Dickinson. See page 47.

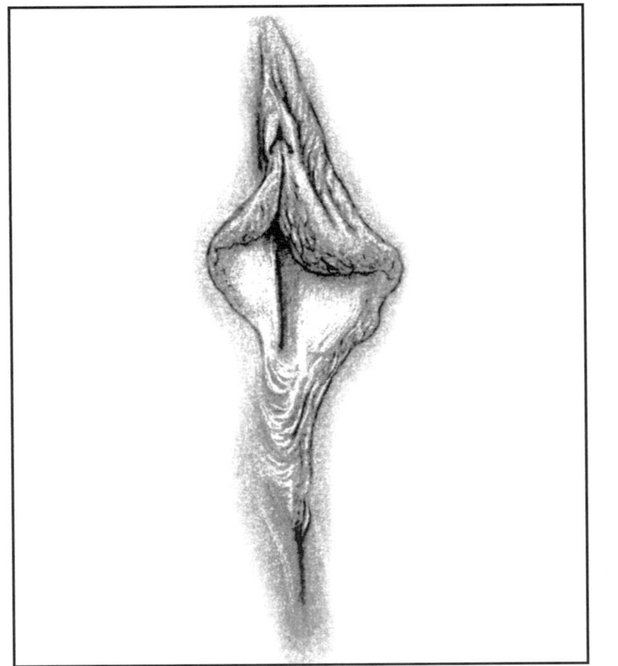

Fig. 23. Diffusely broad labia minora; drawn from life by Robert Latou Dickinson. See page 50.

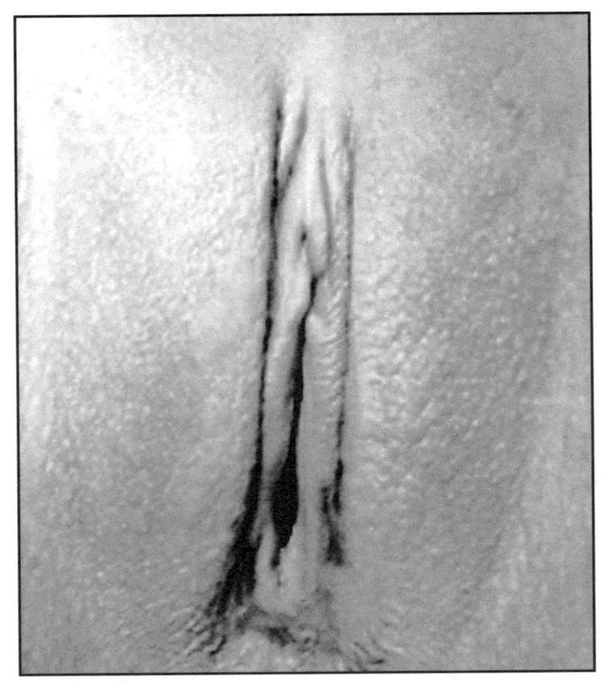

Fig. 24. Diffusely thin labia minora; this is the result of reduction labiaplasty. See page 50.

Colour of the Labia Majora

The colour of the labia majora is related to heredity, so overall skin colour should be taken into account when assessing this feature.

- **Inner surface significantly lighter than outer colour.** A woman who tends to be sensitive, cerebral and contemplative. (See Figure 19.)
- **Deep red or dark, both inside and out:** A woman primarily ruled by her emotion and heart, sometimes stubborn. (See Figure 20.)

STEP 3: READ THE LABIA MINORA

As touched upon earlier, there is great anatomic variation in women's labia minora. They come in all colours, shapes, and lengths, and they change in appearance throughout the course of a woman's life.

Size of the Labia Minora

With regard to labia minora size, my friend Julie Ann Johnson (who is one of the best of all the psychic readers I have ever met) has this important caveat regarding nomenclature:

"Some women may be self-conscious of their large labia minora because scientific anatomists have called them 'hypertrophied' or overgrown. During a physical exam or mantic reading, such long labia should be referred to as 'long, big, wide, and full-fleshed,' never as a 'hottentot apron.'

"The degree of labial spread is, of course, a heritable trait. The term 'hypertrophied labia' was no doubt popularized by scientists who had unknowingly created a false norm when taking their original samples of labial measurement from small-labia races (British, German, Swedish, and Dutch women). Had their research been conducted on African, Jewish, Sicilian, and other ethnicities that often have longer labia, the term might have been reversed, with some parties having 'hypoplastic labia.'

"I tend to call large labia 'fuller' and associate them with will-power. If the labia are small, I say, 'Your labia are very delicate; very refined, like you.'

"And be forewarned! A large labial spread could be falsely identified as a measure of sexual capacity or facility, should one wish — and this 'sexy lips' or pro-labia meme could soon reach far beyond the woman's self-help movement and into the psychic reading community. Be cautious if promoting claims of sexual capacity and facility with respect to large labia!"

Colour of the Labia Minora

Regarding colour, melanocytes are melanin or pigment-producing cells in the skin. A person of dark complexion has more melanocytes in the skin than a fair-skinned person. Skin hyperpigmentation (darkening of the skin) occurs in 90% of all pregnancies, usually in areas where there are more melanocytes, such as the areola of nipples, the umbilicus, the vulva and the perianal skin. It is worth noting that the labia minora may permanently darken in colour after pregnancy. Often, however, the darker colour that appears during pregnancy fades after childbirth.

Exposure of the Labia Minora

One of the major points in the *Genital Horoscope* system of Martha Olschewski is that labia minora size should be measured relative to labia majora size. Without spreading the labia majora, the labia minora are judged to be balanced, mostly exposed, or mostly sheltered.

Exposure or shelter is heritable and is also influenced by overall weight and body habitus or form. Heavier women tend to have more prominent labia majora, and these can envelop the inner structures of the vulva. However, even in women with a normal body mass index, the labia minora can be tucked in between the labia majora and unseen. Women with a large labial spread are unlikely to have their labia minora sheltered by their labia majora.

The first step in the evaluation of a woman's labia minora is to characterize them as (mostly) exposed or (mostly) sheltered. Be aware, though, that sometimes this might not be possible if a woman's body mass index is high.

- **Balanced Labia:** She experiences harmony between cool mentality and emotional states of mind; she does not jump to hasty conclusions.
- **Exposed Labia:** She tends to be intuitive and would like to develop that ability. She has strong will-power, She seems to have always "marched to a different drummer." As an adolescent she probably felt alone; visually sensitive to her environment, she may daydream about a different life in a different place or a different time. (See Figure 21.)
- **Sheltered Labia:** She may have been accused of being "stuck up" or "cold" by those who do not know her well, but really, that isn't the case. Simply, she is complex and other people can't easily figure her out. She feels things very deeply, and aspires to faithfulness. She is more likely to be the one crying in the theater during a sad movie. (See Figure 22.)

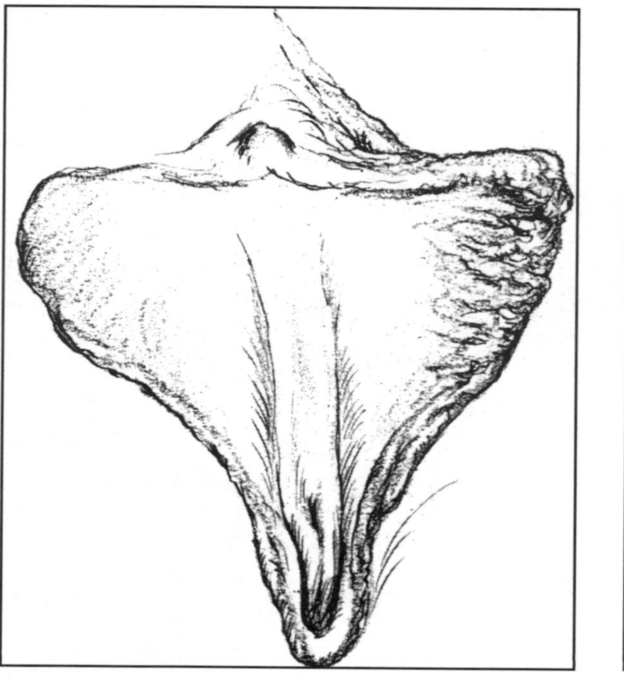

Fig. 25. Broad at the top. thinat middleant bottom; drawn from life by Robert Latou Dickinson. See page 50.

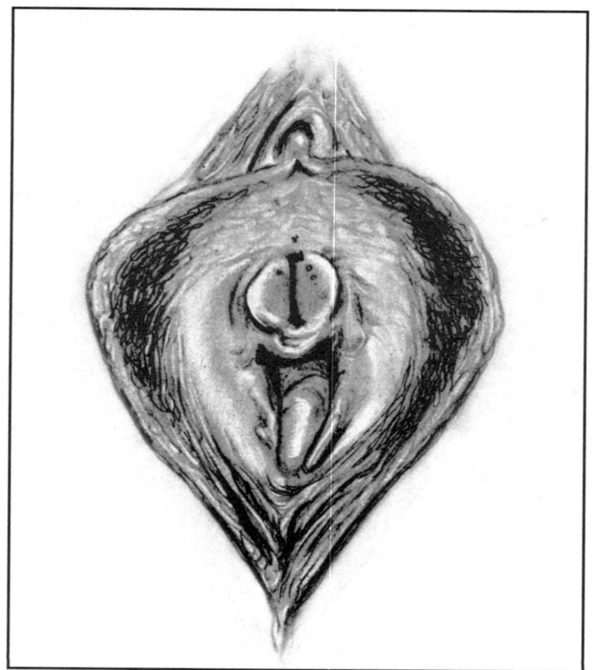

Fig. 26. Broad at the top and middle, thin at the bottom; drawn from life by Robert Latou Dickinson. See page 50.

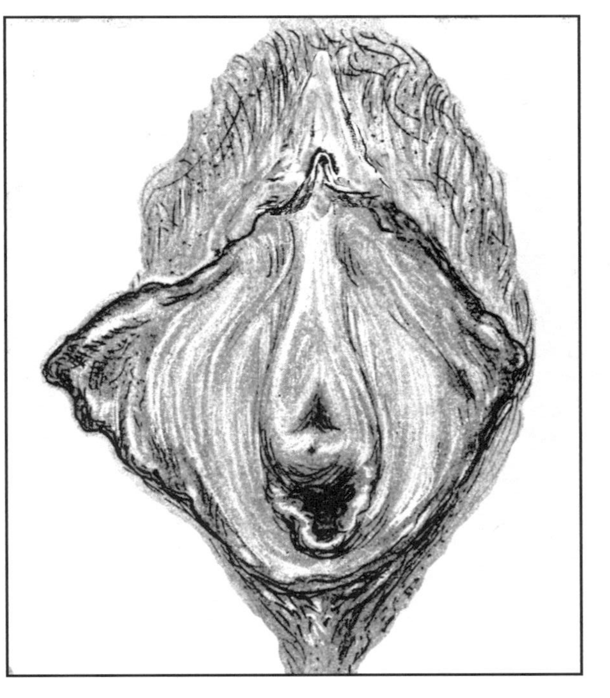

Fig. 27. Broad in the middle, thin at top and bottom; drawn from life by Robert Latou Dickinson. See page 50.

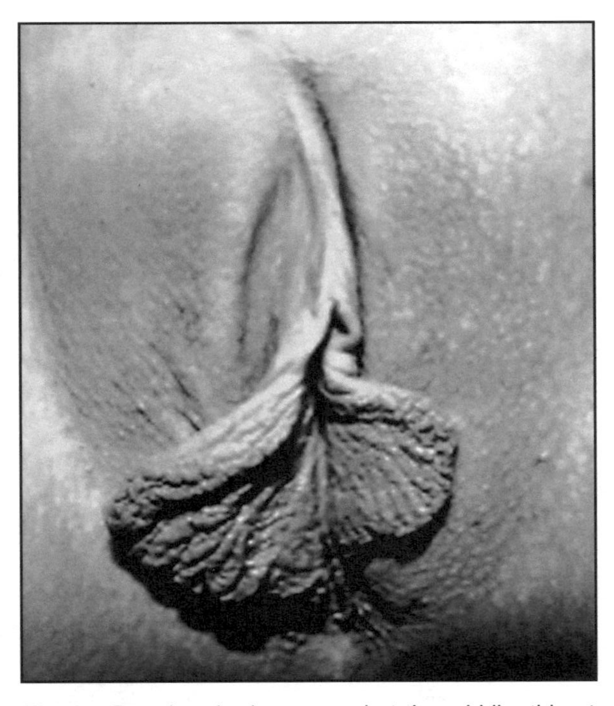

Fig. 28. Broad at the bottom and at the middle, thin at the top. See page 51.

Shape of the Labia Minora

Look at the labia minora as a complete structure and determine if overall they are diffusely broad and full or diffusely thin and narrow. Although most women will not be at either one extreme or the other, understanding these two general shapes will give you a basis for a more detailed reading on the shape of the labia minora:

- **Diffusely broad, full, robust labia:** These women are generally practical, and do not seem to make unrealistic demands of life. When they make up their minds on a subject, all grey areas disappear. They are often perceived as being a little outspoken and opinionated by others, and at times, even a little intimidating. (See Figure 23.)
- **Diffusely thin, narrow and delicate labia:** This physical trait is associated with charisma and charm. These women are diplomatic in speech, with a certain animal magnetism. If not the result of reduction labiaplasty, thin labia are associated with women who have a tendency to gesticulate when they speak. (See Figure 24.)

Very rarely will you see completely full or completely thin labia minora. More common are the mixed types, of which there are five possibilities:

- **Broad at the top, thin at the middle and bottom:** Women whose labia are broad at the top are generally adventurous go-getters. They love to have fun, especially if all the right elements are in place. At times, their love of a good time has gotten them into trouble, but their optimism keeps them upbeat and on the move. (See Figure 25.)
- **Broad at the top and middle, thin at the bottom:** If the labia are broad at the top and at the middle, look out. This woman keeps her cards close. You may not ever really know what she is thinking. Because of this, she is a great secret-keeper, and would make an excellent poker player or even a spy. (See Figure 26.)
- **Broad in the middle, thin at the top and bottom:** Labia that are broad only in the middle are usually associated with an intense, passionate, romantic woman. Do not take "passionate and romantic" as euphemisms for "sexually free or promiscuous." This is a matter of the heart. When this woman loves, she loves with deep intensity, and she generally chooses her mates wisely. (See Figure 27.)

- **Broad at the bottom and middle, thin at the top:** Labia that are broad in both the middle and at the bottom are reflective of a woman who is hard-working and ambitious. She may not be aware of how she got to where she is now, exactly, but she has finally formulated a well thought out goal of where she wants to be in life. She is slowly, cautiously, and purposefully assembling all the right elements in her life to make her big move when the time is right. (See a Figure 28.)
- **Broad at the bottom, thin at the middle and the top:** Women with labia that are broad at the bottom are honest and open-minded. They have a great need for other people to like and admire them. These women are the "salt-of-the-Earth." They don't like lying, and they listen with an open heart and mind. (See Figure 29.)

Symmetry

The final step in labial evaluation is to determine if the lips are even. Surgically altered labia show what the woman aspires to be, not what she naturally is. Also remember that "the client's right labia" is the one on the reader's left, and vice versa, but if the woman is performing a self-reading, her "right labia" is the one on her own right, as might be expected.

- **The labia are even in length:** If both sides of a woman's labia minora are similar in length, no matter which area is broadest, this woman is not ruled by materialism. Rather, she is interested in novel experiences. She is a lover of travel and new foods, and she seeks out exotic and unusual beliefs, as well as friends from diverse cultures. (See Figure 30.)
- **The right labia is longer than the left:** If a woman's right labia is longer than the left, then she is a very generous woman. She is someone who would give you the shirt off her back in a time of need. She is someone whose primary goal is happiness as opposed to money or new experiences. She spends her time trying to better the lives of those around her. (See Figure 31.)
- **The left labia is longer than the right:** If a woman's left labia is longer than her right, then she is or has the potential to be fairly financially savvy. She is likely to be the financial wizard of the house, even if this talent isn't recognized by those around her. Her talent isn't necessarily because of a particular facility for numbers, it is because of her thoughtful financial strategies. She loves a bargain. (See Figure 32.)

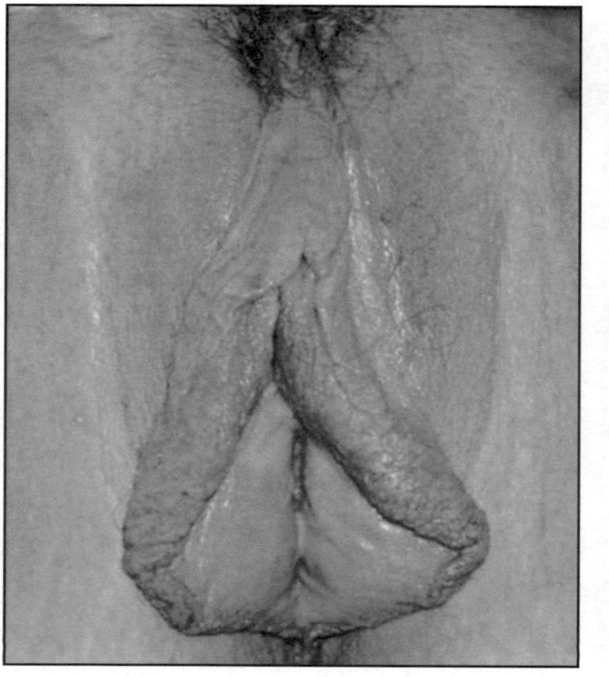

Fig. 29. Broad at the bottom, thin at the middle and top See page 51.

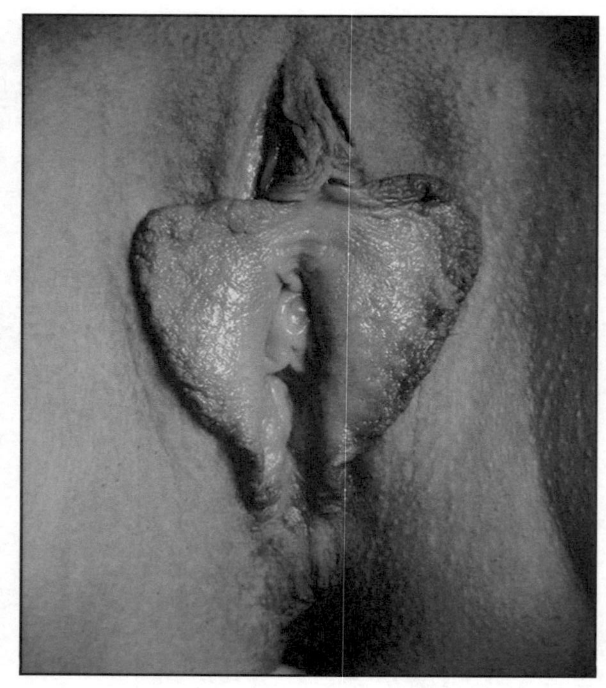

Fig. 30. The labia are very close to being equal or even in length. See page 51.

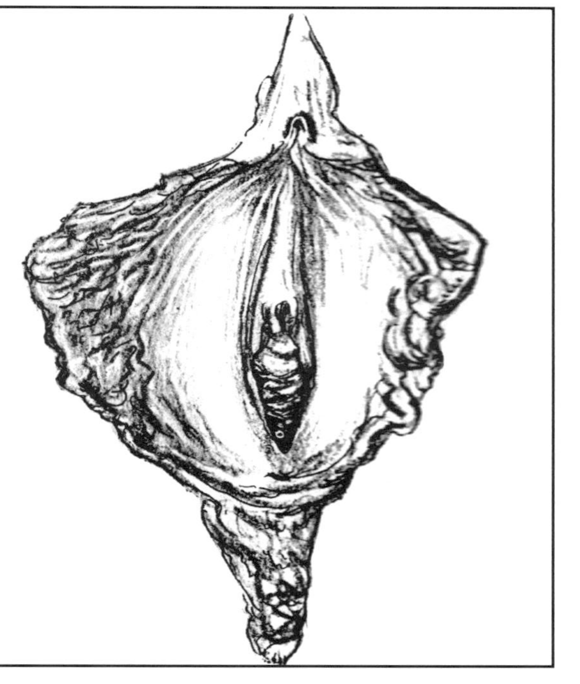

Fig 31. Right labia minora is longer than the left; drawn from life by Robert Latou Dickinson. See page 51.

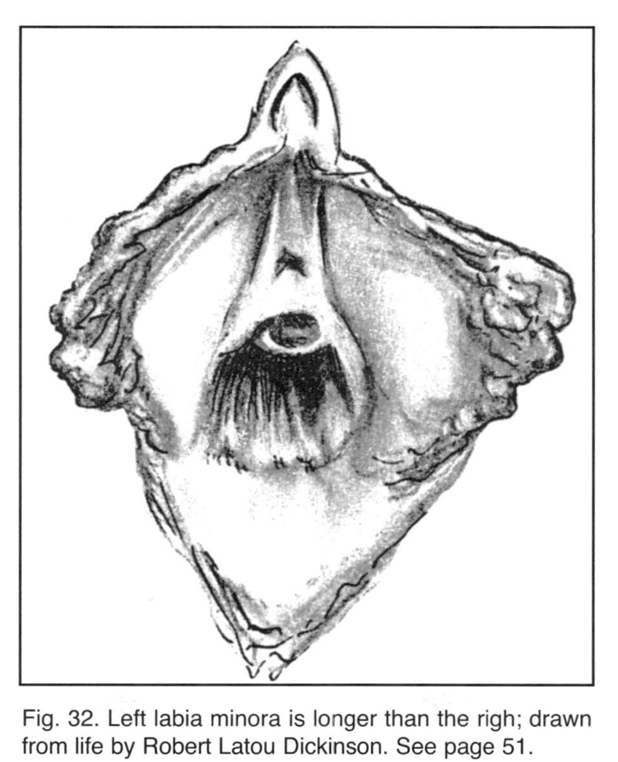

Fig. 32. Left labia minora is longer than the righ; drawn from life by Robert Latou Dickinson. See page 51.

STEP 4: READ THE PREPUCE OR CLITORAL HOOD

The labia minora merge with the prepuce or hood, which covers the clitoral glans in a way similar to how the foreskin covers the head or glans of the penis. Leaving aside the issue of sexual arousal, which can greatly enlarge the glans, we can look to see how much of the glans is covered by the prepuce. Sometimes the glans is exposed, either because it is prominent in size or because the hood is small and only partially covers the glans. Most of the time, the hood just barely covers the glands. Sometimes the hood is fleshy and quite prominent in its own right (the medical term for this is "redundant") and it fully covers all of the clitoral glans.

- **Small Prepuce:** A prepuce that does not cover the entire average-sized glans has been associated with a woman who prides herself to be an independent thinker, someone who does not readily accept others' statements without sufficiency or satisfactory proof. Not quite a skeptic, she is simply someone who has grown beyond her naivete. Such a woman, while generally diplomatic, can sometimes find herself in awkward situations when her ideas conflict with the ruling majority's complacent and unquestioning nature. (See Figure 33.)
- **Average Prepuce:** A prepuce that covers the entire average-sized clitoral glans (so that when retracted, the glans is exposed) is associated with someone who has found it unwise to be too frank in revealing herself to others. At times she can be extroverted, affable, and sociable, while at other times she is introverted, wary, and reserved. She is liked by almost everyone, but only has strong connections to a few individuals. She has one to three like-minded "kindred spirits" and only they know her deepest secrets; sometimes things she wouldn't even share with her husband. (See Figure 34.)
- **Redundant or Large Prepuce:** This signifies a woman who is disciplined and self-controlled outside, but who tends to be worrisome and insecure inside. Sometimes her anxiety gets the best of her and she has what she would describe as a "panic attack." Really it is just a moment of worry that comes and goes "at will" — meaning that no amount of consoling makes the situation better. She has to come to terms with the fact that these episodes just have to pass on their own. (See Figure 35.)

STEP 5: READ THE CLITORAL GLANS

The size of the clitoral glans varies significantly from woman to woman. This can be compared to the way in which the size of a man's penile glans varies — and just as with a man, the size of the glans is dependent on the degree of sexual arousal as well as hormone levels at the time it is measured.

The clitoral glans ranges in size from a little nubbin when flaccid or relaxed to a structure as long as a small penis when fully engorged. When not engorged, a clitoral glans measuring 1-3 mm is considered small; 4-5 mm is average; and above 5 mm is considered large. When the clitoral glans becomes so large that it resembles a small penis, anatomists may refer to it as "penile," although many women find this an unpleasant reference, and prefer the word "extended" to describe it.

You will not be able to read the size of clitoral glans of a woman who is not sexually aroused if her prepuce normally covers the glans.

The degree of pleasure obtained during sexual stimulation is not related to either the relaxed or the engorged size of the clitoral glans.

- **Small Clitoral Glans:** Many readers have associated the small clitoral glans with a woman who is maternal, giving, and protective. This woman has a tendency to be nurturing and loving, sacrificing her needs for the needs of those around her.
- **Average Clitoral Glans:** Both funny and gifted in the visual or musical arts, the woman with a medium-sized clitoral glans finds joy in expressing her creativity. Always a decorator and sharp with colour coordination, she has a great sense of humor and can really make people around her laugh. Sometimes, this can lead to some awkward moments.
- **Large Clitoral Glans:** A large clitoral glans signifies a woman who is punctual and dependable. This woman is reliable. Her self-regulatory ability to be regimented and disciplined inclines her toward athletic sports and other activities that require intense concentration. She makes a good business woman and a long-term friend.
- **Extended or Penile Clitoral Glans:** The penile clitoral glans can be found on a woman who is confident in herself. She resents being pushed around and is not easily intimidated or scared away. She can be very persistent and sometimes demanding, but she is always a "straight shooter" who will tell it like it is. (See Figure 36.)

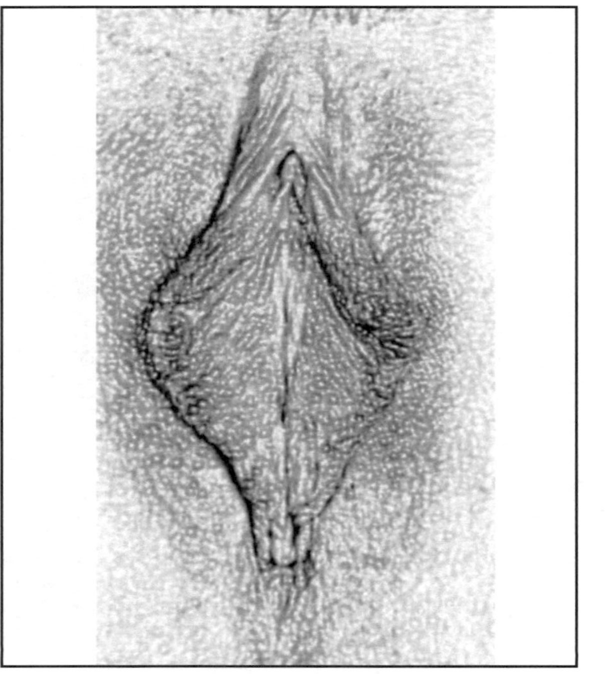

Fig. 33. The prepuce or hood only partially covers clitoral glans. See page 54.

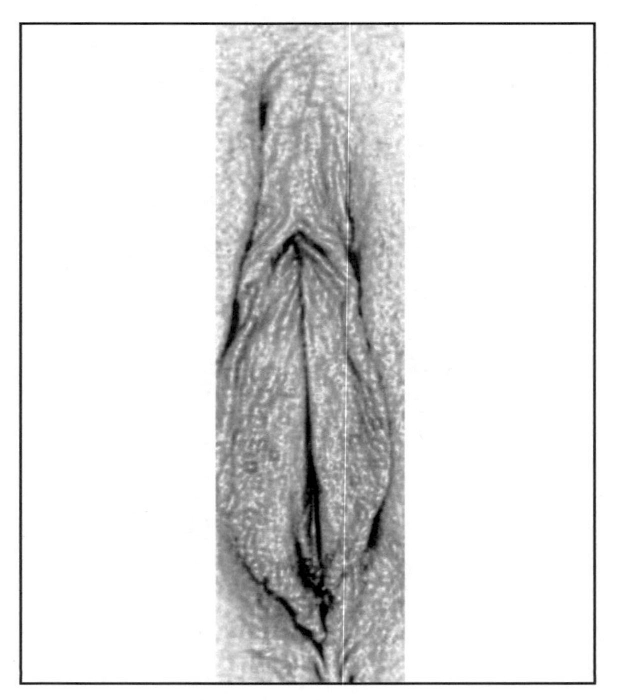

Fig. 34. The prepuce or hood completely covers clitoral glans. See page 54.

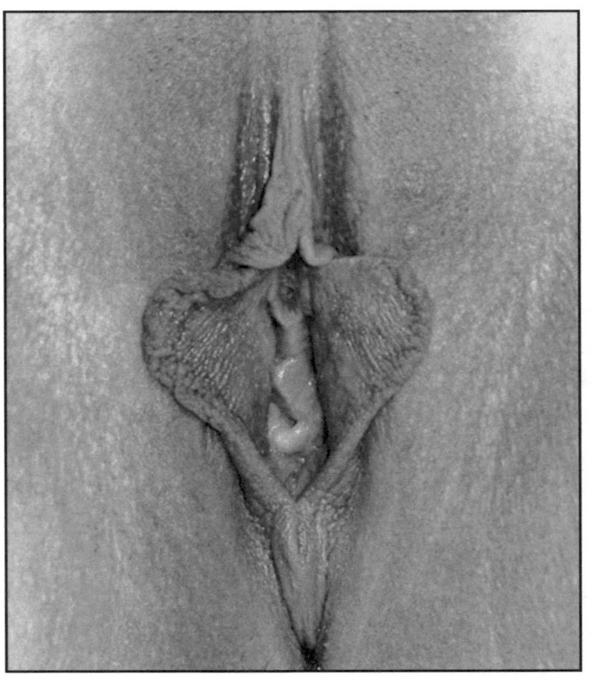

Fig. 35. The prepuce or hood is large and redundant, more than covering the clitoral glans. See page 554.

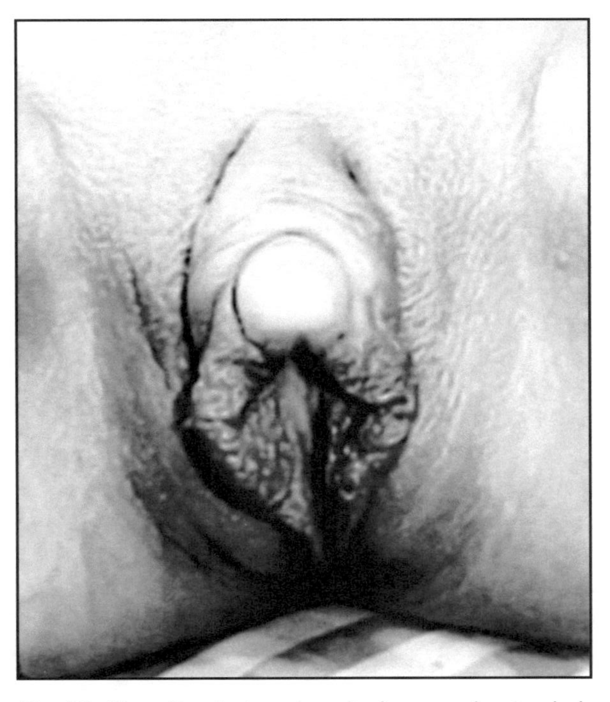

Fig. 36. The clitoral glans is quite large and extended; this is also known as a “penile” clitoris. See page 55.

STEP 6: READ THE SCENT

Eve Ensler, who wrote the famed *Vagina Monologues,* once said:

"My vagina doesn't need to be cleaned up. It smells good already. Don't try to decorate. Don't believe him when he tells you it smells like rose petals when it's supposed to smell like pussy. That's what they're doing — trying to clean it up, make it smell like bathroom spray or a garden. All those douche sprays — floral, berry, rain. I don't want my pussy to smell like rain. All cleaned up like washing a fish after you cook it. I want to taste the fish. That's why I ordered it."

Like wine, each vulva has its own special scent, determined by the bacteria that live in the vagina, diet, type of clothing worn, level of hygiene, bowel habits, how much the woman sweats, and the nature of her own glandular secretions. The glands near the vagina also secrete pheromones, meant to attract a sexual partner.

Ingestion of pineapple or citrus fruits like oranges and grapefruit have been known to sweeten the smell and taste of vaginal fluids. On the other hand, onions, garlic, broccoli, and asparagus can lead to a pungent odour and taste.

- **Little or no scent:** Recently bathed or showered; a cleanly woman.
- **"Musky" odour:** After an athletic workout, there may be a musky odour.
- **"Iron" scent:** The smell of blood signifies menstruation or childbirth.
- **"Yeasty" scent:** When yeast overgrows in the vagina, there may be an odour of freshly baked-bread or a malted beer.
- **"Bleach-like" odour:** Right after intercourse, the faintly bleach-like smell of semen may be detected,
- **"Fishy" odour:** When unhealthy bacteria overgrow, such as in bacterial vaginosis, they release amines, the same chemicals that give fish its characteristic odour. The normal vaginal pH in women of child-bearing age is acidic; below 4.5 and usually 3.8 - 4.2. In pre-menopausal and post-menopausal women, the vagina is mildly acidic to neutral, with a pH of 6.0 - 7.0. Amines have a basic pH, and as amines increase, the normally acid environment of the vagina changes to a more basic pH above 7. This condition is also sometimes accompanied by an off-white, homogenous vaginal discharge, particularly after intercourse.
- **"Perfumey" odour:** She may have dressed herself with oils or used a scented douche; she wants to make an impression.

STEP 7: READ THE DISCHARGE

Changes in hormones during a woman's cycle are reflected in her vaginal discharge. This can give insight into a woman's current state of mind. She may feel emotional or reactive due to changing hormones or maybe exceptionally confident, beautiful, sexy, and empowered.

A normal vaginal discharge consists of about a teaspoon (4 milliliters) a day that is white or transparent, thick to thin, and odourless. Discharge may collect on the inside of the woman's undergarments. Panty readings can be interpreted using the same symbolism used in bed sheet readings, although the marks are not as well-defined and varied as on bed sheets.

Discharge onto undergarments is formed by the normal bacteria and secretions of the cells mixed with vaginal lubrication, urine and menstrual blood. The discharge can be more noticeable at different times of the month depending on ovulation, menstrual flow, sexual activity and birth control. It is not uncommon for the normal discharge to be dark, brown or dis coloured a day or two following the menstrual period.

- **White:** Thick, white discharge is common at the beginning and end of a woman's cycle. It is not accompanied by itching. If itching is present, thick white discharge can indicate a yeast infection.
- **Greyish-White to Yellow:** If accompanied by a "fishy" odour, this may indicate bacterial vaginosis. Two common causes of bacterial vaginosis are having new or multiple sex partners and too-frequent douching.
- **Yellow to Green:** May indicate an infection, especially if thick or clumpy like cottage cheese or if accompanied by a foul odour.
- **Clear and Stretchy:** This is "fertile" mucous and correlates to the time of ovulation. Many women feel particularly confident, beautiful and sexual during this time.
- **Clear and Watery:** This occurs at different times of the cycle and can be particularly heavy after exercising.
- **Blood:** Her period; this is a time of power over men, and the woman is capable of using binding magic to hold or keep a male lover.
- **Brown:** May happen right after periods. Old blood looks brown.
- **Spotting Blood-Brown:** This may occur during ovulation or at mid-cycle. Sometimes early in pregnancy women may have spotting or a brownish discharge at the time their period would normally have come.

STEP 8: READ THE LUBRICATION OR KAMA-SALILA

A women's sexual secretions are comprised of vaginal mucus, lubrication fluid, and cervical mucus. These vary in throughout a woman's life in response to factors such as age, sexual arousal, and cyclical hormone levels.

Vaginal lubrication fluid is the colourless, slick, liquid lubricant secreted by the Skene's glands on the sides of the vulva during sexual arousal.

Cervical mucus originates in the cervix. To the Hindus, it is the "love seed" or kama-salila of a woman, just as semen is the kama-salila of a man.

Kama-salila is at its lowest immediately following a period, and some women report "dryness" during this time. Over the next few days, more mucus develops, which is yellow, cloudy, or white, and somewhat sticky to the touch. As ovulation approaches, cervical mucus increases in quantity and moistness; it may be cream-like in appearance. Immediately preceding ovulation, production of cervical mucus is at its highest and its consistency and colour is similar to egg whites. This fertile-quality cervical mucus, also known as egg white cervical mucus, is clear and stretchy, and is the perfect protective medium for sperm in terms of texture and pH. Having enough egg white cervical mucus during the fertile window improves the chances of conceiving. By noticing when a woman's body is producing egg white cervical mucus, her most fertile days can be identified. Many women find themselves to be more social and more easily aroused at this time.

The most accurate way to identify changes in cervical mucus is to collect a sample from as close to the cervix as possible. The consistency of the sample is tested by rolling the mucus between the thumb and finger, pressing the fingers together, and then slowly moving them apart.

According to the *Ananga Ranga*, each of the four types of yonis has its own distinct kama-salila.

- **The Kama-Salila of a Padmini:** This is described as perfumed like the "lilly, which has newly burst."
- **The Kama-Salila of a Chitrini:** This type is said to be exceptionally hot and abundant; it smells sweet and tastes like honey.
- **The Kama-Salila of a Shankhini:** This woman possesses a kama-salila which is distinctly salty.
- **The Kama-Salila of a Hastini:** This type of kama-salila is said to be mainly musky.

The categories in the *Ananga Ranga* are rudimentary compared to the approach of the modern day vulvamancer. Taste is a complex blend of five distinct groups: sweet, bitter, salty, sour and the more recently identified umami (the savoury taste of glutamates, described as a "brothy" or "meaty" that is long lasting, mouthwatering and coats the tongue). For reasons already described, a woman's kama-salila is dynamic and the changes are subject to the influences of many factors — be they dietary, hormonal, or age-related. They too, may be a reflection of woman's inner state of being.

- **Sweet Kama-Salila:** She was a late bloomer, just now hitting her stride and casting off convention. When she dreams, she generally reports that it is in vivid colours. She is detail-oriented. It is important that the karma-salila is not mixed with sweet urine, which may indicate diabetes.
- **Sour Kama-Salila:** This indicates a woman who had challenges coming to terms with some sexual element of her being. An incurable romantic, she suffered greatly because of unrequited love.
- **Salty Kama-Salila:** She has artistic gifts. Perhaps she tried her hand at poetry or creative writing. Sadly, while the talent is there, time is a factor. In her younger days, she may have undergone a period of depression — even thought about suicide or the affect her death might have on others.
- **Bitter Kama-Salila:** This woman was tied down with responsibility too early in life, either having to step up to the plate as a young family member or marrying too early. She has unfulfilled aspirations.
- **Umami Kama-Salila:** She is constantly busy, sometimes overwhelmed even with her activities of leisure. She has a generally optimistic outlook that is somewhat tempered by the ability to see and power through minor setbacks. She is a woman with significant internal fortitude.

Assuming that one is given permission to taste it, the interpretation of the kama-salila is complex because each woman has the potential to express a unique blend of these five primary tastes, and the vulvamancer must be able to determine which tastes are present and to what extent they predominate. For example, the kama-salila may be strongly salty and sour with a mild component of umami: This woman is an incurable romantic and incorporated her experiences into her art, perhaps writing poetry and stories about a broken love. But she has been working on getting past it. She has the seeds of the strength needed to make it through; however, she isn't quite there yet.

STEP 9: READ THE FEMALE EJACULATE OR AMRITA

Female ejaculation is described as a forceful expulsion of fluid by the para-urethral ducts through and around the human female urethra during or just before an orgasm. How many women ejaculate is unclear, for according to some studies, between 35% and 50% of women report that they have at least once noticed the gushing of fluid during orgasm, while other studies report that between 10% and 69% of women have had this experience. Such a wide range of results may point to flaws in the sampling methods used, including inconsistent definitions of the event; surveys inadvertently or purposely limited to certain populations of women based on age, race, culture, or medical history; confirmation bias or leading questions on the part of researchers; and varying social comfort levels of the respondents with respect to the questioning style of the interviewers or examiners.

Reports on the volume of fluid expelled also vary considerably. The mean reported volume is 1–5 ml. (For reference, the male ejaculate varies from 0.2–6.6 ml and rarely exceeds 13 ml).

The nature of the ejaculated fluid remains debatable as well. Research in this area has concentrated almost exclusively on attempts to prove that the ejaculate is not urine. Why this should be so is unclear, but it again points to confirmation bias on the part of researchers. Practically speaking, since the actual volume of the para-urethral tissue is quite small, larger amounts of ejaculate are likely to contain at least some amount of urine.

Female ejaculate is not a new phenomenon. It has long been known to Hindus as "amrita" — a Sanskrit word which translates to "divine nectar." This term may indicate the roots of the belief that the fluid does not contain urine, for that might belie its divine nature, and indeed, in Western neo-tantra, amrita is considered to be a powerfully healing substance. On the other hand, in Rwanda-Rundi, a Bantu language, female ejaculate is called "kunyaàra" — a word that derives from the word for urine — and it has given rise to a specific sexual technique called kunyaza, in which the urinary meatus is deliberately stimulated during intercourse in order to produce kunyaàra.

Call it what you will, amrita or kunyaàra, readings of female ejaculate can only be performed on the 10% to 69% of women who produce the fluid. As the culmination of a sex magic or neo-tantric ritual, they fall under the heading of bed sheet readings, the symbolism for which is discussed on pages 75 - 78, with referance also to the timing data on pages 69 - 71.

READING SYSTEM SUMMARY

1. Pubic Hair

- Shaved: Fashionable and bold.
- Runway: Trendy but slightly reserved.
- Full and Trimmed: No nonsense, busy.
- Natural: Non-conformist.

2. Labia Majora

- Fleshy / wide: Active and responsive.
- Flat / narrow: Wise from past mistakes.
- Mix: Active and wise.

3. Labia Minora

- Balanced: Harmony between mentality and emotions.
- Exposed: Intuitive, passionate, sensitive to her environment.
- Sheltered: Opaque, quiet, faithful, possessing inner sensitivity.

- Broad overall: Practical and outspoken.
- Broad at the top: Adventurous, fun-loving.
- Broad at the top and middle, thin at the bottom: A secret-keeper.
- Broad in the middle: Passionate, romantic.
- Broad at the bottom and middle: Ambitious, hard-working, cautious.
- Broad at the bottom: Honest and open-minded.
- Thin overall: Charismatic, a leader, possessing animal magnetism.

- Even on both sides: Loves the exotic and unusual.
- Right side longer than left: Generous and giving.
- Left side longer than right: Financially talented.

4. Prepuce or Clitoral Hood

- Hood with exposed clitoris: Independent thinker.
- Hood with clitoris covered: Affable, well-liked.
- Redundant hood: Inner worrier.

5. Clitoral Glans

- Small: Protective, nurturing.
- Medium: Funny, artistic.
- Large: Punctual, disciplined, athletic.
- Penile: Confident, demanding.

6. Scent

- Little or no scent: Cleanly woman.
- "Musky" odour: Athletic.
- "Iron" scent: Menstruation or childbirth.
- "Yeasty" scent: A yeast infection.
- "Bleach-like" odor: Has recently had after intercourse.
- "Fishy" odor: Bacterial vaginosis.
- "Perfumey" odor: Wants to make an impression.

7. Discharge

- White: Normal, but with itching indicates a yeast infection.
- Greyish-White to Yellow: "Fishy," multiple partners, over-douching.
- Yellow to Green: An infection, often with a foul odor.
- Clear and Stretchy: Fertile, confident, beautiful and sexual.
- Clear and Watery: May have recently beenexercising.
- Blood: Period, a time of great power over men.
- Brown: Period has just passed.
- Spotting Blood-Brown: Ovulation or early pregnancy.

8. Lubrication or Kama-Salila

- Sweet: Late bloomer.
- Sour: Sexual issues, unrequited love.
- Salty: Artistic, a sense of sadness (past or present).
- Bitter: Unfulfilled aspirations, held back.
- Umami: Busy, intense, has internal strength.

9. Female Ejaculate or Amrita

- Present: Read the bed sheet, using the symbolism on pages 75 - 78.
- Absent: No reading is possible.

A SAMPLE READING

Putting It All Together

Using the summary, let's work out a reading for an imaginary woman:

- **A highly groomed runway pubic hairstyle; no piercings or tattoos**
- **Flat and wide labia majora**
- **Exposed labia minora**
- **Labia minora broad at the top, thin at the middle and bottom**
- **Left labia minora is slightly longer than the right**
- **The hood covers her clitoris**
- **The clitoral glans is medium in size**
- **Her scent is minimal**
- **Her discharge is clear and stretchy**
- **Her kama-salila is dominated by a blend of umami and bitter**
- **She does not ejaculate amrita**

This is a trendy woman, fashionable and well put together, who resists wearing gaudy colours or ostentatious jewelry. She has been through hard times and is the wiser for it. She is active, and there are not enough hours in the day for her to accomplish everything she would like to do.

Appreciated by her peers as a great conversationalist, she doesn't share everything with just anyone. She has one or two close friends and, if she doesn't already have yearly getaways with them, she would greatly benefit by doing so. While she is well-liked, it may take time for people to really see her for who she is — a deep soul who is often moved by the plight of others, a very empathic woman.

She loves adventure, and in her eyes nothing beats laughing with people. She saves her money and budgets wisely. Perhaps she even has more than one account, maybe a rainy-day fund or a retirement account. She loves laughter, has a quick wit, and is known for cracking a good joke. She enjoys and creates art in her limited spare time.

She is clean and has a professional appearance. In her tender moments, she will reveal how much she would love to have a child. She is a busy woman who needs to carve out some "me time" for her art. Saddled with responsibility too early in life, she pushed forward and overcame the hurdles of her past. She is now coming to a more stable equilibrium in her life.

Changing a few things will change the reading

It is important to take note when a woman has more than one physical characteristic that is associated with a similar personality trait.

For instance, in the example above, had the woman's right labia minora been longer than her left and her clitoral glans small in size, her self-sacrificing nature would be particularly strong and should not be undervalued — and had she evidenced the "bleachy" smell of recent intercourse, her fertile egg white mucus may have indicated that her desire for a child was on its way toward immanent fulfillment.

How to Handle Anatomical Complexities During the Reading

Let us consider a few of the anatomical complexities that can confound the novice vulvamancer.

- **Difficulties with anatomic interpretation:** How does one evaluate the length of the labia minora? Are the labia minora truly sheltered? Does the prepuce really cover the clitoris or is this a transient state? The solution to problems stemming from questions about female anatomical landmarks is simply to perform more readings. Expertise is achieved through study, practice, and mentorship by an authentic yoni reader.
- **Difficulties with implied conflicting characteristics:** If a characteristic implied by one anatomical feature is contradicted by another, this is not evidence that the system is wrong. Rather it indicates that the client herself may grapple internally with opposing personality traits. For instance, in certain circumstances, a woman may be gregarious and in another environment she may be shy and introverted. Likewise, a woman who has been a strategic saver for her retirement may go on spending sprees once in a while. Learn to read both traits together as a narrative.
- **Difficulties with non-standard genitalia:** Interpretation of intersex anatomy caused by genetics is beyond the scope of this text, but you are encouraged to give it a try. Female genital mutilation presents a different problem, for the client may have missing structures and, tragically, may be unaware of what was done to her. Avoid any expression of shock and proceed as best you can or, if you suspect that she is ignorant of the extent of her impairment, kindly refer her to a gynecologist. The same is true for a woman who shows evidence of serious infection, cysts, or tumours; advise her to get a medical exam.

SELF-READINGS FOR WOMAN

The most accurate readings by an experienced and legitimate vulvamancer are given in person. The reader may be female or male, and it goes without saying that the reading should be conducted from a place of client safety and not as an excuse for inappropriate or unwanted sexual contact. (This is not to say that readings between consenting sexual partners cannot be sexy — of course they can!) However, not every woman is comfortable allowing a reader to examine her vulva. Therefore, she may opt to provide a photographic picture, a series of pictures, or a short cell-phone video of her vulva to the reader. This is a well-accepted "second-best" option.

Some women may be uncomfortable even providing an image of themselves even to a legitimate vulvamancer, or they may not be able to locate one. Some are simply self-curious and want to test this system on themselves, much like people who buy a palmistry book to check out their own hands. In all of these cases, women are fully able to read themselves by using a mirror.

Self-reading the vulva resembles the well-known self-examination techniques that many women have learned do with a large hand-held mirror in order to monitor their vaginal and pelvic health. However, although a self-exam requires physical flexibility, a speculum, and good distance vision, self-reading, which might seem to be a cumbersome and awkward process, poses fewer challenges to those with limited mobility or low vision, due to smart-phone camera technology. Currently, most phones include a camera with enough resolution to glean all the information necessary to make an accurate yoni reading.

Because the pictures taken with the phone need to substitute for direct visualization, it may be necessary to capture the vulva from several different angles. These would include the vulva at rest, the vulva with the labia majora gently spread and the vestibule exposed, the labia minora gently spread, and a photo with the hood retracted in order to expose the glans of the clitoris.

Whenever a camera or a mirror is employed in self-reading, it important to preserve sidedness information correctly, because sidedness can change the outcome of a reading if the vulva is asymmetrical. One way to be sure which side is which is to put a dot of lipstick or a small pen-mark on the skin of the right inner thigh.

A COMPLETE YONI DIVINATION SYSTEM

Only a few people in the world have sufficiently mastered yoni divination to the extent that they can call themselves legitimate vulvamantic fortune tellers by observation of the body alone. Current day vulvamancers instead often practice divination with objects that have been in close contact with the vulva. This form of vulvamancy includes effluvia-based panty, menstrual pad, ceromancy pad, and bed sheet divinations, plus tampon pendulum divinations and specially prepared cowrie shell divinations to obtain answers to questions about the woman's past, present, or future.

All of the effluvia methods are grounded upon an understanding of the symbology associated with visual patterns, the same as might be observed in tea leaf, speal bone, candle-glass, and cloud interpretation, as well as in crystallomancy, pyromancy, mirror-scrying, and dream interpretation.

In vulvamancy, not only the images, but also the nature of the effluvia should be taken into consideration, for menstrual blood, urine leakage, amrita, mingled semen and vaginal fluids, feces, and hairs have meanings in and of themselves. For example, red menstrual blood is active, brown is stable, and black is gloomy. Hairs point to important images and also indicate good luck or talent in magic. Mingled male and female fluids imply that the divination might best center on the outlook for love and marriage.

PANTY DIVINATION

Panties are intimate apparel, and as such, using them for divination requires tact and delicacy. However, some women too shy for a yoni divination may feel comfortable sending their panties to a fortune teller.

Start by treating the panties as you would the vulva: smell them.

Next evaluate them as æsthetic objects. Interpret the fabric (cotton is plainer than latex or silk) and the colour (white for purity, buff or brown to mimic skin tones, black for seductiveness, red for sex, and other colours to harmonize with outerwear). Observe any images or words written on them.

Make note of how the panties were acquired: did the client send them or did her lover or spouse steal them from the laundry hamper?

Finally, examine them for signs or marks of vaginal discharge, post-coital fluids, urine, or feces. Interpret these signs according to meanings on page 64, the symbology on pages 75 - 78, and the timing data on pages 69 - 71.

MENSTRUAL PAD DIVINATION

Early forms of menstrual protection included knitted pads, strips of folded cloth, and menstrual aprons. All of these have been used to foretell future events. The practice of menstrual blood divination may go back to the ancient Jewish Niddah laws. Niddah is a Hebrew term for a woman during or after menstruation who has not yet undertaken purification by immersion in a mikveh or ritual bath. To ascertain that her period is through before entering the mikveh, she must undertake a self-examination with a bedikah ("checking cloth"), also called an eid ("witness") in Hebrew.

What you will be observing in a divination of this type are the shapes left on the pad at the time it is given to you to interpret. The shapes will suggest images, and the images will reveal traditional symbolic meanings. The pad need not be "fresh' — the images will remain as if painted for a long time.

When did the period begin?

Start by asking the time of day, day of the week, and date of the month upon which menstruation commenced. Note the meanings of these times.

The time of day that the period began:

- Periods that start in the morning relate to love. It can be a romantic love for a specific man or woman or the deep but platonic love of a family member or close friend. It may even be heart-love of a pet.
- Periods that start in the afternoon express positivity and happiness.
- Periods that start in the evening bring boredom and ennui; sometimes apathy will be the main mood during the entire next menstrual cycle.
- Periods that start at night symbolize loneliness or loss. There may be a feeling of disappointment in those on whom you closely depend.

The day of the week that the period began:

- Monday: Worry, concerns, planning, lists; feelings of falling behind.
- Tuesday: New events, changes, unexpected surprises, confrontations.
- Wednesday: Episodic bouts of calm reassurance punctuate this cycle.
- Thursday: Opportunities for introspection and self betterment.
- Friday: Susceptible to frustration and impatience, especially in love.
- Saturday: Positivity with bursts of creativity; a sense of justice.
- Sunday: Fatigue, lack of motivation, or, conversely, relaxation.

The day of the month that the period began:

1: Feelings of contentment and satisfaction.
2: Someone or something will make you disgusted.
3: Arguments. Try to be careful to avoid a conflict.
4: Increased sensitivity. Overstimulation. Distraction.
5: Surprise. Something unexpected. A gift.
6: Overwhelmed, over-committed, and over-emotional.
7: Self exploration. Self-realization. Self-empowerment.
8: Jealousy. Envy. Beware of false friends.
9: Worries related to reputation. Gossip.
10: Romantic concerns, changes, and transitions.
11: Laughter and humor, good cheer and joy.
12: Charisma. Excitement. Sexuality, art, and music.
13: Loyalty. Commitment. Sustaining power.
14: Professional challenges. Frustration or change.
15: New adventure. A new start. Clean slate.
16: Travel, either by yourself or friends.
17: Abandonment. Loss. A setback of some kind.
18: Financial concerns and opportunities.
19: Unrequited feelings. A missed connection.
20: Feelings of malaise, illness, and low immunity.
21: Be careful. Treachery is afoot. Test the spirits.
22: Inability to focus. Loss of concentration. Clumsiness.
23: Strength, ether physical, mental, or spiritual.
24: Insecurity. Second guesses. Indecisiveness.
25: New persons are encountered. A friendly stranger.
26: Forgiveness. A good time to re-connect.
27: Spirituality. Oneness. Acceptance. Unity.
28: Self-assuredness. Business or relationship plans.
29: Sadness, sometimes for no apparent reason.
30: Confidence. Security. Stability in friendship or love.
31: Time to act. Aggression. Self-defense. Determination.

Take note of special dates

If the period began on a solar or lunar eclipse, conditions are stalled. Astrologers will know not to divine menses when the Moon is Void of Course.

If it is the client's birthday, you may tell her fortune for the entire year.

Timing by location of shapes on the pad

As with other forms of divination, event timing may be determined with menstrual pads. In tea cup interpretations, timing moves clockwise and down. Patterns that touch the rim are "now," after which the reader works through the shapes in a downward spiral. The first spiral is "a week from now," the second spiral is "two weeks from now," the third spiral is "three weeks from now," and, finally, "one month from now" is at bottom center of the cup. With pads, the system is much simpler, as it derives from the old three-card cut found in cartomancy, also called the past-present-future cut. To use it, mentally divide the pad into thirds and note the locations of the shapes:

- **Anterior pad imprints:** The front of the pad is what the woman is walking into. Symbols here represent her immediate future. If positive, she welcomes what is foretold. If negative, she may feel anxiety.
- **The middle of the pad:** This what she is experiencing now. Depending on the symbol, it may be a present problem or it may be a comfortably stable situation, condition, or relationship.
- **Posterior pad imprints:** The rear end of the pad is what she is walking away from. Symbols here represent events of the recent past or situations and relationships that she wishes to put behind her.

Special menstrual pads

Some menstruations are more significant than others:

• **The first menstrual pad:** You must not interpret a young girl's first menstrual pad, for she is below the age of consent.

• **The first menstrual pad after marriage:** The bride may seek a divination on the outlook for her marriage. Pay particular attention to patterns that symbolize love, conjugal happiness, or partnership difficulties.

• **The post-partum pad:** Bleeding after childbirth is not menstrual; the discharge is called lochia ("related to childbirth" in Greek) and it consists of clotted blood and tissues shed from the uterine lining. It may persist for weeks. Focus attention on symbols relating to motherhood, and if you see very large clots or much fresh blood, advise the client to seek medical care.

• **The last menstrual pad:** The last menstrual pattern to be produced by a woman who has entered the final stage of menopause is said to give insight important to the entire next chapter of her life.

CEROMANCY PAD DIVINATION

Not all women have menstrual cycles. For post-menopausal women, women who have undergone a hysterectomy, women who are on a form of birth control that prevents the onset of a period, or women who have questions that are too pressing to wait for their menses, there is an alternative method of divination — the ceromancy pad divination.

Ceromancy, is the art of divination through the use of wax, most commonly candle wax. As explained by Catherine Yronwode in *"The Art of Hoodoo Candle Magic,"* there are two types of ceromancy.

- **Dripping:** A candle is lit and as it burns, its wax is dripped into cold water, snow, or sand. The hardened wax shapes are read like tea leaves.
- **Melting:** A candle is lit and the way in which it melts, as well as the forms taken by the wax remnants in the holder, are observed for signs.

We will use the first form of ceromancy, in which the wax is dripped from the candle — but rather than catching it in water, snow, or sand, it will be dripped onto a menstrual pad.

You will need a red candle, preferably a vulva-shaped candle of the type that can be obtained from an occult shop, and from one to six fresh and unused menstrual pads.

If you will be doing a yoni reading before the divination, light the candle when you start the reading and it will be burning when you begin the divination. If the divination is all you will be doing, light the candle about one hour before the divination is to begin and use the time to focus your attention on the questions to be asked and to prepare the menstrual pads.

Lay out one pad per question or concern. Write each question on the back (non-absorbent side) of one pad with a red marker. Turn the pads over on the table with the absorbent side face up, and, similar to tarot cards, give them a "wash" — that is, mix them on the table. Then spread the pads out on the table like a clock, with the front end of each pad toward the center.

With the vulva candle elevated about six inches from each pad, drip wax onto each pad, starting at the twelve o'clock position and moving clockwise in an circle. Each pad should receive roughly the same quantity of wax in an irregular pattern. Each pad's question is then answered by means of the interpretive symbol system used for conventional menstrual pad divinations.

BED SHEET DIVINATION

Like panty, menstrual pad, and ceromancy pad divinarionss, bed sheet fortune telling employs visual symbology in the construction of an interpreted narrative of present and future events. In this case, what is being observed for signs is the patterns made by effluvia such as menstrual blood, post-coital fluid, lochia, or amrita upon the sheets where the woman has reclined, made love, delivered a child, or slept.

As explained by Nagasiva Yronwode, who largely developed this system of divination for his own use, there is an orientation to the bed sheet; that is, it has a head and a foot. The "head" relates to thoughts, the "heart and hand" to emotions and works, and the "foot" to travel and domination over others. Additionally, if a couple shares a bed, each may have a favoured sleeping side, and these locational cues are taken into consideration as well.

Predictive bed sheet divinations may be undertaken upon a virgin's first sex act, when blood from her hymen conveys divinitory meanings. In some cultures, the simple presence of such blood is taken as a sign of "consummation of the marriage," and the sheets are displayed to the family as proof that the marriage is valid. However, a skilled vulvamancer will also interpret the blood pattern as a prediction of the success of the marriage.

If the diviner is attending upon a childbirth, there is also the opportunity to observe amniotic fluid and lochia. Interpretation of amniotic fluid patterns is conducted similarly to bed sheet divination, but when lochia and amniotic fluids combine, the prediction may have to do with either the mother or the child. In this case, the subject of the divination can be identified by correct interpretation of the symbols found on the sheet.

Bed sheet divination may also be employed by participants in neo-tantric pujas who seek connection to a deeper spirituality through their pleasure and union. The natural time for interpretation is after the completion of the ritual. Menstrual blood and the amrita produced through masturbation can be read after monofocal rituals, while post-coital fluidic divination with any number or combination of fluids are suited to duofocal or polyfocal rituals.

In sex magic, the focus is to harness the sexual energies produced during climax, so a natural time for divination would be at the completion of the sexual act that results in the production of the fluids. A bed sheet divination after sex magic will be useful to predict the progress or outcome of any spell-casting tied to the sex act or energetically broadcast during orgasm.

TAMPON PENDULUM DIVINATION

According to Michæl Weber, tampons that have absorbed menstrual blood can be used as pendulums to divine the future. Common questions asked of the tampon pendulum are those regarding love, health, fidelity, and fertility of the woman. She herself maybe the client or the tampon may have been surreptitiously acquired for use in learning more about her.

The pendulum should be suspended no more than an inch above the table, with the elbow on the table. A basic yes / no / maybe chart or an alphanumeric chart can be used, or the diviner may work freehand. If a chart is used, often the pendulum will be stilled at the start, and if it swings in a particular direction, this becomes the baseline and the chart is aligned with the baseline. Alternatively, the pendulum is "told" or "trained" to understand the operator's "yes," "no," "maybe," "and I don't know," after which it is stilled and questioning begins. All questions are addressed by name to the tampon pendulum as if to the woman herself.

COWRIE SHELL DIVINATION

The mantic art of casting Cowrie shells is worth briefly mentioning. Due to their natural form, the shells are taken to be symbolic representations of vulvas and thus foretelling the future them forms a parallel and indirect divinatory art that complements direct yoni or pad divination.

The word "porcelain" comes from the Italian "porcellana," which translates as "Cowrie shell" and refers to porcelain's similar shiny surface. "Porcellana" in turn comes from "porcella," a sow piglet, because the shell resembles a small female Pig. Additionally, the sawtooth "lips" of the shell are associated with the mythical "vagina dentata" or toothed vulva.

Cowrie shell divination is popular in African and Afro-Caribbean cultures. In a religious context, only priests interpret the elaborate array of 16 Cowries called diloggun, with its 256 possible outcomes, but simple 4-shell obi readings, which produce 5 results, may be undertaken by lay people.

Julie Ann Johnson's unconventional yet effective spell-casting method to directly link a set of 4 of these vulva-like shells to a specific woman in order to perform distance forecasts about or for her can be found on page 93.

Read more about how to interpret obi shells in this book:
"Throwing the Bones" by Catherine Yronwode

FLUIDIC SYMBOLS AND THEIR MEANINGS

Airplane: Long-distance journey; a rise in social position.
Anchor: At top, stability and rest; at bottom, safety.
Angel: Protection from negative influences. A seen or unseen ally.
Animals: Meanings center on their commonly accepted characteristics.

- **Bat:** Swiftness in action or change.
- **Bear:** Strong protection and nurturing.
- **Cat:** Independence, agility, self-reliance. Also gossip or deceit.
- **Cattle:** Cow: Nurturing motherhood. Bull: Strength, stubbornness.
- **Dog:** A good, true friend; at bottom, a friend needs help.
- **Dolphin:** Uncommon talents and abilities.
- **Fish:** Increase of wealth, increase in family, new ideas.
- **Fox:** Treachery by a trusted friend or an unsuspected enemy.
- **Goat:** Playfulness. Beware of stubborn people.
- **Horse:** Energy. Progress. Galloping: news. Horse head: a lover.
- **Lion:** An influential friend in a position of authority.
- **Mouse:** A small theft, probably due to inattention.
- **Octopus:** Danger at sea.
- **Pig:** Greed and carelessness. Luck for the New Year,
- **Rabbit:** Need for bravery to overcome a fear of disaster.
- **Rat:** Treachery, dishonesty.
- **Sheep:** Good fortune. A warm and helpful friend. Gullibility.
- **Snake:** Dealing with someone you do not like. Wisdom to discern.
- **Squirrel:** Save up now for future times of want.
- **Tortoise or Turtle:** Slow, steady progress. A sluggard near to you.
- **Whale:** Intuition and connections with others. Great wisdom.
- **Wolf:** Cunning, wildness. A loyal friend or a predatory enemy.
- **Zebra:** Adventures overseas.

Arrow: Whole: Events happening quickly. Broken: Events delayed.
Axe: Difficulties and divisions; if at top, overcoming of difficulties.
Baby: Children, youth. Small joys. If fretting, small worries.
Bag: An unknown item; if closed, a trap; if open, escape from a trap.
Ball: Variable fortunes, like a ball bouncing up and down.
Balloon: A celebration or party soon.
Basket: A treat, an award. Holding onto things, saving, keeping.
Bell: Announcement of happy news, possibly a wedding or promotion.

Birds: Good news is on the way. Waiting for a message.

- **Chicken:** Hen on nest: wishes come true. Rooster: brave courage.
- **Dove:** News of love and proposals of marriage.
- **Duck:** Money, and false gossip about money.
- **Eagle:** Success over obstacles.
- **Egg:** If unbroken, success; if broken, failure.
- **Feather:** Lack of concentration; insincerity, undependability.
- **Hawk:** Be watchful; suspicion and jealousy are found in inferiors.
- **Ostrich:** Travel abroad; hiding from unpleasant events.
- **Owl:** A wise person, teacher, coach, or mentor will help.
- **Raven:** Bad news; disappointment in love; death for the aged.

Boat: A visit from a friend. Freedom to travel.

Book: Learning, classes. Open: good news. Closed: there are secrets.

Boot: Work, sustained effort.

Bottle: Drunkenness, possible addiction problems, also medicine.

Bow (Ribbon): Celebration. A gift.

Box: The unknown, because the contents are unknown.

Broom: A new home or a thorough house-cleaning.

Candle: Ask for and receive help from others. Someone may love you.

Chain: A sequence of events. A physical or psychological addiction.

Chair: A guest is coming, prepare a place. Relaxation.

Circle: Success, completion. If near dots, a baby on the way.

Clock: Don't procrastinate. Something needs fixing right away.

Clouds: Trouble, pessimism. With rain drops near, problems or tears.

Coin: Money is coming; the number of coins shows how much.

Cross: Death, a funeral, suffering, sacrifice, a crossroads.

Crown: Honours gained. A person of authority.

Crutch: Some assistance is required.

Cup: A reward of merit. Emotions. Love, affection.

Dagger: Danger from self or others; beware of injury.

Diamond: Money, possessions, reward, payment.

Dish: Trouble at home; matters require cleaning up.

Dress: Appearance, fashion, and social relations.

Envelope: Good news. With dots near, news of money.

Ear: You need to listen; you may be missing a message.

Eye: Psychic ability, introspection. Look sharp. Wake up!

Face: If known, that person. If unknown, a change, perhaps a setback.

Fan: Flirtation, but it comes to nothing in the end.
Fence: Limitations, minor setbacks, easily mended.
Footprint: First steps, beginnings. Persistent memories.
Fork: False flattery, lies being told.
Gate: Opportunity, future success, removal of obstacles.
Ghost: Haunted by the past. A fear from the past.
Glass: Water-glass: integrity. Cocktail glass: dissatisfaction.
Hammer: Hard work is needed; avoid complainers.
Hand: If open, a friendly helper; if closed, an argument.
Heart: Love, pleasure, romance, caring, a thrilling meeting.
House: Security and safety; parents; home improvements.
Insects and Arachnids: Minor problems require immediate attention.

- **Ant or Bee:** Group effort for the collective good. Social media.
- **Butterfly:** An admirer who will lose interest quickly.
- **Fly:** Domestic annoyances may require your attention.
- **Spider:** Good luck, industriousness, a reward for work.
- **Wasp:** Your romantic problems are due to a rival.

Jewels: Gifts will be offered to you; don't be vain.
Key: The answer you need. Keyhole: More information is needed.
Kite: Ascent in social position through the help of friends.
Lightning: Unplanned sudden changes beyond control or even prediction.
Loop: Avoid too much imagination, over thinking, or worry.
Moon: Things are changing, beware of illusion and self-deception.
Mountain: Great goals. Possible achievement requires determination.
Pen or Pencil: The written word. Ideas.
Plants: Meanings center on their commonly accepted characteristics.

- **Acorn or Oak:** At top, slow, steady growth. At bottom, good health.
- **Apple:** Achievement; if bitten, temptation, secret knowledge.
- **Fern:** Dignity, peace in the home, steady love.
- **Flower Bouquet:** Emergent development, blossoming as a person.
- **Forest:** Quiet, peacefulness. Alternatively, exploration.
- **Grapes:** Health, fertility, happiness; if with a bottle, inebriation.
- **Leaf or Leaves:** Something that is diminishing or going away.
- **Palm:** Tree: Success, victory. Leaf: honour, martyrdom.
- **Pine Tree:** High achievement and notability.
- **Rose:** Flower: Love, affection. Bush: A secret.
- **Sunflower:** Optimism, renewal.

Plus Sign: Two people or two situations; events joining together.
Purse: At top, profit; at bottom, loss through carelessness.
Question Mark: Be cautious; the future is unsettled.
Rainbow: The most difficult time is now over.
Rain Drops: Tears, regrets. If raining on plants, fertility.
Ring: At top, marriage; at bottom, betrothal. Broken: divorce.
Scales: Legal issues. If balanced, justice; if unbalanced, injustice.
Scarecrow: Feelings of loneliness.
Scissors: Quarrels, possibly separation or alienation.
Shell: Good news, heard second hand. Good news from over the sea.
Ship: At top, a worthwhile journey; at bottom, a safe journey.
Shoes: Opportunity, a new venture. Hard work leads to betterment.
Sickle: Illness, sorrow, pain, and death.
Skull: Danger. Something toxic. Death.
Spade: Conflict, argument, clashes. Conscious choosing or comparing.
Spiral: Going within or growing outward.
Spoon: Generosity. Sharing.
Square: Protection. Reliability. Consistency. Stability.
Stairs: Becoming more aware. Career advancement or promotion.
Star: Success, luck. Reward that seems unearned.
Sun: Renewed energy. Happiness, success, power, children, well-being.
Sword: Conflict, argument. Logical thinking.
Table: Social gathering or celebration at which you'll find favour.
Teardrops: Sorrow. Regret. Loss.
Tent: Travel for which you are not well prepared.
Thimble: Friend or acquaintance needs assistance. A need for mending.
Top Hat: An expert; a lawyer, a doctor, a judge, an official authority.
Tower: Unexpected chaos, disappointment, and possible ruin.
Triangle: Something unexpected will happen soon.
Umbrella: Trouble from which you will be protected.
Vase: A friend needs your help.
Violin: A musical interlude; a self-centered person.
Volcano: Harmful emotions; take action to change or limit these.
Waterfall: Prosperity. Fading of nagging or guilty feelings.
Wheel: Movement. Transport. Someone returns. Broken: disappointment.
Window: New point of view, new ideas, new information.
Wings: Need to get away, if only temporarily. Messages from Heaven.

SAMPLE DIVINATIONS

Be aware of the various intrusions that can complicate the interpretation. An IUD, menstrual cup, or contraceptive sponge are examples of extrinsic factors that can impact flow and pattern. Recent intimacy or particular activities during the pad's collection are also liable to distort or heavily shape the result. Intensity of flow, solidity of emission, colour at the time of evaluation (red, brown, or black), and the observation of any other features, such as hairs, semen, or tissue should be noted.

Putting It All Together

Let's work out a couple of quick divinations for an imaginary woman. This method applies to panties, menstrual pads, ceromancy pads, or bed sheets:

- **Her period began on Monday, the 3rd of the month, in the morning.**
- **A scissors shape at the front / top**
- **Three small droplets (raindrops) at center**
- **A sickle-shape at the back / bottom**
- **The fluid is dark, almost black, and there are no inclusions**

This woman has had an illness or someone close to her may have died, but she is recovering. She still is very sad when she thinks of it. She will soon be cutting off a relationship, perhaps with family members, perhaps with her partner. She is ready for this time of sorrow to end.

- **Her period started Tuesday, the 16th of the month, in the evening.**
- **A ring at the front / top, and a plus sign of two crossed hairs near it**
- **Nothing at the center**
- **A pair of wings at the back / bottom**
- **The fluid is red, and a faint string of tissue forms part of the ring**
- **Her second period after this one will fall around her birthday**

This woman has been feeling bored and out of sorts. She wishes to travel, but the blank center means it will take at least one more menstrual cycle before she can leave. The second period after this one is her birthday period, a great time to begin something new. In fact, while travelling, she may meet and cast a love spell on the one whom she is to marry!

VULVAMANCY IN NEO-TANTRA

WHAT IS NEO-TANTRA?

Tantra yoga comprises esoteric and exoteric Hindu and Buddhist religious rites that incorporate five antinomian sacraments: parched grain, fish, meat, wine, and sexual intercourse, either visualized or physically present. Set against culturally normative vegetarianism and celibacy, these rituals derive much of their charge from their transgressive nature. Chinese Taoist sexual alchemy, which uses similar rites, has as its goal the practitioner's immortality.

When 19th century Europeans "discovered" tantra yoga, they got no thrill from what seemed to be its boringly mundane restaurant fare — after all, what British traveller had not already eaten roasted corn, fish, or meat, or had a glass of wine? Sex alchemy's promises they dismissed as fantasy. "Oriental" sexual intercourse, however — that was worthy of further investigation! So, blinded by cultural hegemony, they reduced tantra yoga to "sex religion" and sexual alchemy to "sex magic," and then celebrated them as such.

Asian religious sexuality was studied by Victorian hobby anthropologists and social reformers like Paschal Beverley Randolph, Clifford Howard, Hargrave Jennings, Alice Bunker Stockham, John Humphrey Noyes, George Washington Savory, A. E. Newton, George N. Miller, and J. William Lloyd. Under names such as "Sex Worship," "Eulis," "The Better Way," "Male Continence," "The Anseiratic Mysteries," "Zugassent's Discovery," "Bosom Love," "Karezza," "Phallism," and "Magnetation," they taught the mystical aspects of sexual intercourse. These books were often privately printed to avoid prosecution under laws that forbade the distribution of sexual images or descriptions of birth control. Some referenced Asian veneration of the yoni as a justification for publication, but Hinduism, Buddhism, and Taoism were eclipsed, while Christianity, Spiritualism, and New Thought came to the fore.

In the 1970s, Asian religious sexuality again made the rounds in the West. The earlier list of inventive names had been forgotten, and "tantra yoga" was the term of choice, but again the Western focus was primarily on sex. This time, however, Hindus complained about the mischaracterization of tantra. By the 1990s it was understood how disrespectful and culturally inappropriate it is to describe non-Hindu rites of sex veneration as "tantra yoga." Thus the term "neo-tantra" was devised. A complete misnomer —it is not new and it is not tantra — it might better be described as "Asian influenced sacred sex."

THE AIMS AND PURPOSES OF SACRED SEX

Let's start with some disclaimers:

- Vulvamancy will not teach you authentic Indian tantra yoga, either of the "right hand" or "left hand" path. For that, it is recommended that you seek out core source texts such as the *Yoni Tantra, Maya Tantra, Gandharva Tantra, Nila Tantra, Brhannila Tantra, Sarvavijai Tantra,* or *Kularnarva Tantra,* and work with a Hindu teacher.
- Vulvamancy will not teach you authentic Chinese sexual alchemy. For that, it is recommended that you seek out core source texts such as *The Art of the Bedchamber,* and work with a Taoist teacher.
- Vulvamancy will not teach you authentic old-school American methods of sacred sex. For that it is recommended that you seek out core source texts such as *Eulis: the History of Love, Karezza: Ethics of Marriage, Hell Upon Earth Made Heaven,* and *The Karezza Method.*
- Vulvamancy will not teach you the most enjoyable and healthful sexual techniques. For that, you may seek out popular and reputable resources such as *The Alt.Sex FAQ* at LuckyMojo.com/faqs/altsex online.

Spiritual connections through intensified sexuality is central to the practice of all forms of sacred sex. It is known that climax is a complex physiological process involving neurotransmitters, hormones, changes in blood flow, and transient changes in the perception of space and time. Obviously, repeated orgasm, lengthening of the time spent experiencing orgasm, and increasing the intensity of orgasm will heighten and prolong these physiological changes. In fact, using these techniques, one can induce altered states of euphoria similar to those that people try to attain through feats of endurance, meditation, pain, and drug use. In the altered states of consciousness brought about through the practice of sacred sex, one may experience not only delayed and more powerful orgasms, but also increased intimacy, self-knowledge, self-empowerment, and even enlightenment.

It should be noted that although traditional tantra rites place emphasis on the union of male and female, modern neo-tantra, karezza, and sacred sex rituals are equally applicable to gay or lesbian sexual union.

Read more about the varieties of sacred sex here:
LuckyMojo.com/tktantradefinition.html

TO COME OR NOT TO COME

For 150 years in America, proponents of various types of sexual mysticism have been divided in their opinions about what role — if any — the orgasm plays in sacred sex. The roots of this disagreement go back many centuries.

Surprising as it may seem, the old Hindu tantras and Taoist sex alchemy treatises teach us nothing about the female orgasm at all. Avoidance of male orgasm is important in these texts, because ejaculation is thought to deplete sacred sexual energy, while reserving semen provides amazing benefits — but women, without visible erections to master or physical bindu or seed to hold back, are simply to be venerated; the female orgasm counts for nothing.

In the 19th century, John Humphrey Noyes followed down this same path, developing a sacred sex technique he called "male continence," in which "the male inserted his penis into the vagina and retained it there for even an hour without emission, though orgasm took place in the woman."

Alice Bunker Stockham, on the other hand, promoted gender parity in karezza. She wrote that every sex act should begin with a mystical dedication, and that women can reap spiritual benefits by controlling their orgasms just as men do. She taught that after days or weeks of "quiet union" without orgasm, both parties might gently reach mutual climax. Her student J. William Lloyd went a step further; he gave control of the sex act over to the woman entirely so that the man could avoid the "accident" of unplanned ejaculation. Another of Stockham's colleagues, George Washington Savory, urged men with fertile wives to ejaculate between their breasts, to avoid pregnancy.

Meanwhile, Paschal Beverley Randolph, always an original thinker, took a wildly different approach. Preaching against "the murderous habit of incompletion of the conjugal rite" through coitus reservatus, he warned that while choirs of angels attend upon couples who breathe a prayer at "the nuptive moment" and experience holy mutual climax with each and every sex act, those who withhold climax for any reason attract legions of demonic and vampiric spirits to their bedrooms, and go down to an early grave.

Somewhere amongst all of these sincere theories, you will find the method that suits you. No matter what it is — from "celibate intercourse" to mutually magnetized one-hour orgasms — you can be assured that someone has experienced it, and has written an impassioned book about it as well.

Read more about the history and techniques of American sacred sex here: **LuckyMojo.com/sacredsex.html**

VULVAMANCY IN NEO-TANTRIC YONI PUJAS

The yoni puja ceremony honours the vulva. This can be a symbolic yoni of a statue or the yoni of a living woman. Different schools of neo-tantric study incorporate different elements in their particular yoni pujas. A puja may involve making offerings of food and drink while chanting prayers. It may involve the deliberate sexual arousal of a woman who is believed to embody or personify the goddess. Yoni puja rituals help participants attain sexually-induced spiritual enlightenment and enhanced sexual enjoyment and further strengthen bonds and relationships in both the physical and spiritual realms.

Both the character readings and the divinatory predictions of vulvamancy can be incorporated during yoni puja ceremonies. The pujas are generally performed in a ceremonial temple or in a sacred space created with specific intent to honour the yoni. It should be peaceful and safe. Arrange enough time for ritual, and take care that you will not be disturbed or interrupted in any way.

The sacred space should be both immaculate and inspiring, a place of worship and the stage of the ceremony. The bed chamber is usually kept warm, generally around 80 degrees. Since neo-tantra is a celebration of life, it is celebration of all senses. Therefore, the sacred space has offerings of candles and flowers that are pleasing to the eye and sense of smell. There are edible fruits, sweets, and libations, meant to engage the the sense of taste. The aroma of holy incense or perfume permeates the air.

This yoni puja consists of eight rituals: sacred washing, the ritual of reverence, the ceremony of the yoni reading, the rites of touch, blessed love, the ritual of union, the dance of the divine, and the bed sheet interpretation.

PART 1. SACRED WASHING

The yoni puja ceremony starts with a ritual washing of the earthly personification of the female energy (Shakti) and the male energy (Shiva). Both bodies are washed and cleansed gently and lovingly. During this time Shakti and Shiva cleanse their heart and mind. Worries, sorrows, and all negative thoughts and emotions are washed away with water. The water may be clear or it may include flower petals or Siva Sakti Bath Crystals. The female and male energies allow themselves to become open and receiving, both pure and innocent. When this state is achieved, the participants dress in light ceremonial robes that are used only for this purpose.

PART 2. RITUAL OF REVERENCE

In this ritual, the aim is to truly see the divine in your partner, and to feel it in yourself.

After the sacred washing is concluded, the robed Shakti and Shiva energies meet each other openly, face each other with love, and gently take one another's hands. The words, *"The divine in me greets divine in you"* are spoken; in Sanskrit, this entire phrase is a single word: *"Namaste."* You may say it in Sanskrit or in English, as you prefer.

Now focused on each other, Shakti and Shiva lock eyes and seek to see and feel the divine in one another, as well as in themselves. This sacred moment, the meeting of divinities, is achieved as the representations of Shakti and Shiva synchronize their breathing, align their energies, perhaps their heartbeats, and ultimately, their thoughts. To the goddess or god, the other becomes a manifestation of the divine and of the cosmic Feminine or Masculine. As synchronicity occurs and the two are in perfect spiritual alignment, there may be a palpable change in warmth within the yoni of the goddess and in the corresponding lingam of Shiva.

It is at this point that Shakti and Shiva, possessors of the yoni and of the lingam, may exchange small tokens of their holy connection to each other. The gift is the physical representation of their union. In some pujas, the gift is as simple as a flower or handmade token. Amongst the dedicated practitioners other tokens of love may be exchanged, such as a spotted Cowrie shell, a small Shiva lingam stone, an Indonesian mamoli or womb amulet, a Thai palad khik or penis amulet, or an Irish Sheela Na Gig pendant depicting a woman opening her yoni. (See Figures 37, 38, and 39.)

The gift excange is done in silence. Appreciation and thanks are communicated mentally with real, loving energy devoted to appreciate the thoughtfulness, tenderness, and consideration of the giver and of the receiver.

After a period of meditative thanks, the holy communion of food and libation begins. While still sitting close to each other and touching gently, Shakti and Shiva hand-feed each other bite-sized morsels of foods chosen specifically for their varied tastes and textures as well as for their aphrodisiacal properties. They also offer one another small portions of celebratory libations. As Shiva serves Shakti, Shiva is serving the divinity in himself. As Shakti serves Shiva, she serves the divinity in herself. Thus, the energy created is amplified by each feeding of the other.

PART 3. CEREMONY OF THE YONI READING

Shakti lays down upon an elevated "mandura" or comfortable mat or cushioned surface. If necessary, it may be pre-heated with hot water bottles.

Lifting her robe, Shakti positions herself into a modified Baddha Konasana yoga pose. Rather that the typical "bound angle" pose, this is performed lying down, feet together, knees apart and supported by pillows.

It is at this point that Shiva gathers the information needed for the yoni reading. As the reading is performed and recorded, Shakti alternates between two mudras. A mudra is a spiritual gesture and an energetic seal of authenticity, generally made with the hands. Each mudra activates a specific effect on the practitioner. The five fingers symbolize the five Asian elements:

The thumb symbolizes fire
The index or pointer finger symbolizes wind
The middle finger symbolizes ether
The ring finger symbolizes earth
The little or pinky finger symbolizes water

The first mudra is the yoni mudra. The hands are held in prayer position, palms together and opposing fingers aligned. The fingers are then splayed apart and the ring fingers are folded in and crossed. Pressing the little and middle fingers together with the ring fingers crossed, the base of the thumbs, the index fingers, and the palms separate, as if opening the wings of a butterfly. The index fingers then hook behind the crossed ring fingers, and the thumbs are pressed back together, touching the bases of the middle fingers. The yoni mudra brings about calmness and helps increase mental focus.

The shakti mudra follows. While keeping the little fingers together and the middle fingers together, the ring fingers are released and held together. The middle fingers are then separated, after which the hands are widely separated so that only the ring and little fingers can still touch. The thumbs are folded in towards the palms and the index and middle fingers are then folded over the thumbs. The shakti mudra releases tension in the pelvic region.

The yoni reading is recorded by Shiva on vellum with permanent Walnut ink, which carries mystical meaning in ancient India. Once the reading is completed and recorded, the rites of touch is started. The reading is only given to Shakti at the conclusion of the puja.

PART 4. RITES OF TOUCH

For this rite you need pre-warmed massage oil made with 8.66 ounces (the mystical number of the vesica piscis) of Grapeseed oil plus 8 drops of Siva Sakti Oil. You also need to know that in Hindu spiritual theory, the body is said to have seven chakras or disks arrayed along the spine, from the first or root chakra at the sacrum, up to the seventh chakra at the top of the head.

Shiva begins the massage at Shakti's seventh or crown chakra, gently holding the thumbs in place while the finger tips trace a slow wavy-fluid motion from where they naturally rest toward the center of the chakra.

The thumbs next touch the sixth chakra or third eye on the forehead. The fingers lightly press the temples with a circular motion. The salivary glands beneath the jaw are caressed with a milking motion. The receiver accepts the touch, relaxes, and lets all tension disappear. Shiva says aloud, "Trust the touch of others, feel reverence and love in it. You are now safe and loved by the divine. Shiva is caressing and touching you now. Let the divine love you."

After moving down the arms to the fingertips of Shakti's hands Shiva's left hand touches Shakti's left shoulder and, once placed, the right hand lets go of Shakti's fingertips and joins the left hand. Shiva next massages Shakti's fourth chakra, between the breasts, and then the third chakra of the abdomen is lightly caressed and kneaded.

PART 5. BLESSED LOVE

Shakti and Shiva look into the eyes of one another and focus on seeing the divine in each other. Bodies are caressed and the words, "We are all sacred and beautiful. Body is our holy temple." are spoken. Eventually, fire, passion, and desire awaken in both Shiva and Shakti and, when ready, Shiva enters inside of Shakti through the holy temple of the second chakra.

PART 6. RITUAL OF UNION

While Shakti is in the embrace of Shiva, both begin to breathe and move in the same rhythm, feeling connection and love, as both focus on the present moment until past and future become indistinguishable,and they achieve specific desired spiritual states, be they of oneness, harmony, mental focus, awareness, healing, or movement to a higher plane.

PART 7. DANCE OF THE DIVINE

When Shakti and Shiva dance together, the flow of energy will grow and expand. Love is made consciously. At that moment of climax, Shiva and Shakti feel oneness, energy, power of life, flowing freely between them.

PART 8. BED SHEET DIVINATION

At the conclusion of the Dance of the Divine, a vulvamantic bed sheet divination can be made, and it too should be recorded with Walnut ink. If the puja was performed with a specific goal in mind, the interpretation may speak to it. For instance, if the goal was to achieve a connection with ancestral energies, the divination may provide a message from ancestral spirits.

WALNUT INK FOR USE DURING YONI PUJAS

Roman myth gives us Walnut tree's botanical genus name, Juglans, for it was said that Jupiter, the king of the gods, also known as Jove, lived on Walnuts when he lived on earth. Juglans means "Jove's glans," like the glans of the clitoris or penis. In India, to dream of a Walnut is highly symbolic It may foretell difficulties due to its hard shell, but to dream of opening and eating one means difficulties will be overcome. Dreaming of nuts can also signify wisdom, for the nut resembles a human brain, and it also represents sexuality, for it looks like a testicle but also, internally like a vulva.

These associations make Walnut hulls, either from Black or English varieties, ideal for use as ink in the recording of readings and divinations. Oxidize the hulls by gathering them in the Fall, and keeping them outside in a sealed glass container until January. Put them in water in a large caldron and simmer for 4 - 6 hours on low, then strain off the liquid and discard the hulls. Pour the liquid through a fine sieve to further and then simmer it without boiling until the volume is reduced by half. Strain the resulting concentrated liquid though a finely-woven cotton cloth, allowing it to drip through naturally without squeezing. Test the consistency to be sure that it is perfect for writing with a fountain pen or a calligraphy pen. Simmer longer if necessary, Add 1 tablespoon plus 1 teaspoon of 99% isopropyl alcohol per quart of strained, concentrated walnut dye, as a preservative. The ink is permanent on any type of paper, once it has dried.

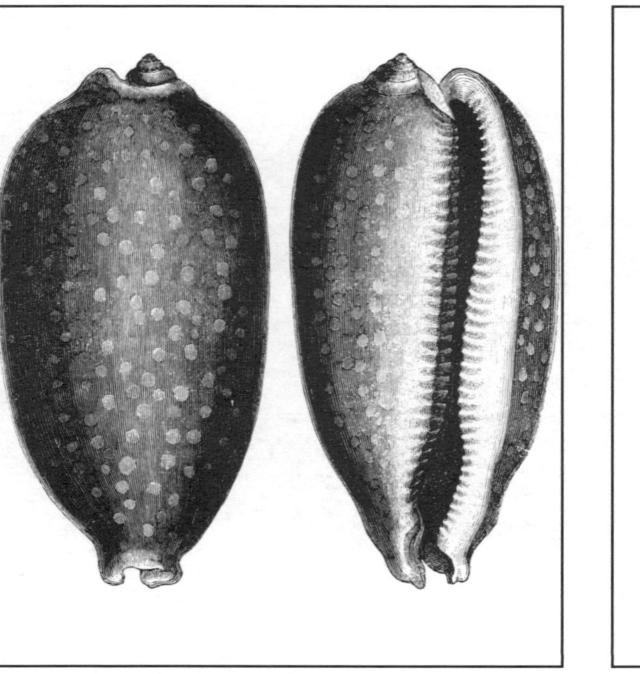

Fig. 37. The shells of Cowries are almost universally taken to represent the yoni in folk magic. See page 84.

Fig. 38. Mamoli amulet from Indonesia; it represents the vagina and womb in cross-section. See page 84.

Fig. 39. Sterling silver Sheela-Na-Gig pendant; an Irish image of a woman holding her yoni open. See page 84.

Fig. 40. The vesica piscis in the lamen or pendant worn by members of the Ordo Templi Orientis. See page 91.

VULVAMANCY IN SEX MAGIC

WHAT IS SEX MAGIC?

Magic is the art of influencing the course of events and producing change in the world through non-causal, mysterious, or supernatural means, such as witchcraft, hoodoo, rootwork, enchantment, or spell-casting. Sex magic refers to magical pursuits or spell-casting techniques that incorporate sexual activity or sexualized imagery. Sex magic may include an act of intercourse or masturbation, or it may be performed with symbols and curios evocative of a sex act.

When an actual sex act is part of the magical work, bodily movements may be ritualized, orgasm may be withheld or utilized as part of the work, and the desired outcome may be visualized during the activity or at the moment of climax in an attempt to harness and direct the energy of sexual arousal or orgasm and focus this energy to achieve the hoped-for result.

THE AIMS AND PURPOSES OF SEX MAGIC

The aims of sex magic can be sexual, as when it is utilized to influence someone's sexuality, love, or fidelity. Its aims can also be non-sexual, as when bringing the power of sexual excitement to bear upon a sought-after non-sexual outcome, such as physical healing or enhanced clarity of mind.

ALICE BUNKER STOCKHAM AND SEX-MAGICAL PRAYER

Some people do not consider prayer to be a magical act, while others believe it is a way to change the world. Be that as it may, the concept of prayer as magic is an important part of the sacred sex methods of karezza. Alice Bunker Stockham and J. William Lloyd both taught that karezza's coitus reservatus techniques would provide mundane benefits such as birth control (they opposed abortion but wanted women to control pregnancies), social and political equality for women (they felt that "karezza men" would never rape or harm their wives), and increased marital pleasure and hence marital fidelity (they taught that karezza is a cure for "failing marriages"). However, they also advocated using the withheld orgasm as a moment to pray for physical healing and for lofty charitable goals such as world peace.

PASCHAL BEVERLY RANDOLPH AND MODERN SEX MAGIC

The earliest known practical teachings of sex magic in America come from the 19th-century occultist Paschal Beverly Randolph. As a person of colour and a world traveller, he embraced both down-home African-American conjure and European ceremonial magic. A well-respected Spiritualist medium and stage lecturer who promoted hashish as an aid to trance induction, he also made and sold love powders, consecrated scrying mirrors, and "the New Orleans Magnetic Pillow" for sexual happiness, fidelity, and dreaming true.

Randolph was an advocate of mutual orgasm in the rites of the anseiratic mysteries of eulis, his name for sacred sex, and with his first wife he made use of their resultant conjoined sexual fluids in the manufacture of love potions, remedies, and sachet powders. He also mixed the mingled fluids with lactucarium, an opioid derivative of Lettuce, and used this to paint sigils on the backs of convex scrying mirrors. The sigils were then covered over with black paint, the mirrors were placed in gilded frames, and the resultant goods were sold for use in divination by his mail order clients and students.

ALEISTER CROWLEY AND CEREMONIAL SEX MAGICK

In the 20th century, Western sex magic was influenced by the writings of Aleister Crowley, the man who popularly put the "k" in magick. Born in England in 1875, Crowley was an openly bisexual occultist, which was unusual during his era, but he was also a drug addict, an elitist, and a cynical social critic who supported racist and sexist agendas. Despite having been labelled a satanist and "the Wickedest Man in the World" in the press, he attracted many followers and remains an influential figure among members of the Ordo Templi Orientis, a fraternal order which he led, and which incorporates a vesica piscis in its emblem. (See Figure 40.)

Crowley identified sex as the most powerful force in life and considered it to be the supreme source of magical power as well. He advocated masturbation, homosexuality, and sadomasochism as components of sex magic and he also attempted to fuse European magic with Asian magical techniques. Some of his texts on sex magic have been published and made available to the general public and some have been kept secret and released only to initiates of his Ordo Templi Orientis lodges.

VULVAMANCY IN CEREMONIAL SEX MAGIC

Just as yoni readings and divination are incorporated into neo-tantra, they may also be used in the modern practice of ceremonial sex magic.

TALISMANIC SEX MAGIC RITUAL

Talisman are objects that have been consecrated and charged with specific energy. Whether purchased from a spiritual supply house or crafted by oneself, the talisman is specific to the ceremony, so a talisman meant to attract luck may look quite different than one intended for protection or good health.

Not all talismans are prepared during rites of sex magic, but it is well-known that talismans may be employed to contain, focus, and direct the energy created during a ritual sex act toward a specific purpose. In this example, we will prepare a talisman for the protection of a home.

Before the rite begins, the magician bathes. Specific herbs, perfumes, oils, or colourants are added to the water to focus the magician's energy and purge unwanted energies. Basil, for instance, protects the home.

A special area is selected for the ritual. Candles and incense mark the ceremonial space. In accordance with common colour symbology, white candles are used for attracting a new or unknown lover, red arouses passion or restores nature, black is to wreak sexual vengeance, and blue signifies peacefulness and a happy home. Therefor blue would be chosen for this rite.

A preparatory ritual of banishment is performed. Because the generation of magical energy is thought to attract spirits, the banishment clears the ceremonial space of any unwanted forces. Banishment rituals vary in their origins, and there are numerous effective banishment rituals in print.

The talisman is put on a small offering plate. Erotic simulation begins and various sexual positions, acts, and techniques are employed to increase and intensify the power until a final orgasm is achieved. A bed-sheet divination is then made with specific inquiry into the outcome of the work.

If semen, vaginal fluid, menses, or amrita are produced during the sex act, the talisman is charged by a transference of the fluid(s) to the talisman. Any remaining fluid is added to wine and a closing banishment is performed. If the talisman is to be worn or carried, the wine is consumed, but since this talisman is intended to protect the home, it may be buried in the yard and the charged wine poured on the ground over it as a libation.

VULVAMANCY IN FOLK MAGIC SPELLS

Not all sex magic derives from ceremonial or ritual magic; much of it developed in folk magic usage around the world.

COWRIE SHELL VULVAMANCY CONSECRATION SPELL

Julie Ann Johnson is a spiritual advisor whose techniques combine traditional forms of divination and spell-casting. Here she shares a way to use obi shells to divine about or influence a woman at a distance

"Obtain a set of 4 of the cut Cowrie shells used in obi divination. These are not whole shells, but sliced ones, specifically used for readings.

"To link the shells to a woman without her being aware of the link, secretly collect her menstrual blood or vaginal fluids. For example, find a used tampon and soak it in water to extract the blood. Prepare or dress the shells with the fluidic extract each evening for one lunar cycle, from New Moon to New Moon. Keep the fluid in the freezer in between times of use, as it is biodegradable. For best results, place a photo of the woman beneath the shells and pray or call her name as you work.

"If the woman is a willing partner in the venture, explain what you will be doing and ask her to consecrate the shells by wearing them in a single-layer cheesecloth wrapping-pad in contact with her vulva for one full menstrual or lunar cycle. She should bleed, urinate, or drip sexual fluids through the shells. The cheesecloth may be changed daily for the sake of freshness. It may be removed briefly for sexual intercourse, if swiftly replaced.

"At the end of the lunar or menstrual cycle, the shells will have absorbed a great deal of her prepotent power and will be thoroughly linked to her. They can then can be used when she is distant, to surreptitiously answer questions about her mental, emotional, physical, or social state or to perform vulvamantic divinations on her behalf, with her consent.

"The readings are obi divinations, for which instructions can be found in books such as *'Throwing the Bones'* by Catherine Yronwode.

"To cast a spell that will produce an effect on the woman at a distance, with or without her consent, lay the prepared shells out on a surface in a selected obi pattern or a naturally cast pattern that suits your purposes, then use them to surround an appropriately coloured vulva candle dressed and lit for attraction, love, sexuality, reconciliation, healing, or harm."

CONCLUSION

This book should serve to give you a good start in all four branches of vulvamancy: character analysis, foretelling the future, reading the character and foretelling the future during a rite of sacred sex, and divining while performing ceremonial magic or folk magic spells.

You may not desire to become a professional certified vulvamancer; you may just want this knowledge for personal use. Perhaps this mantic art will serve you well in your private life when you wish to learn more about a lover or a potential mate. Perhaps it will provide a springboard for intimate discussions with your mate or help you to bring into focus your goals and intentions with respect to sexuality. Maybe vulvamancy will enhance the richness and quality of your relationships. All of these goals are certainly within anyone's grasp.

At its least complex, this book may simply become a volume of not-quite-smutty oddities to you, something to share with like-minded friends. But do not take it too lightly, because as many before you have found out, expertise in vulvamancy can also be a useful adjunct to genuinely mystical practices, both sexual and non-sexual.

As your interest grows and you outgrow this book, I hope that you increase your knowledge through practice and mentorship. If a reputable vulvamancer is not available to teach you, then it is my intention that the lengthy bibliography provided with on the following pages should give you useful pointers toward a wide array of ancient and contemporary texts that deal with the anatomical, medical, cultural, political, mystical, religious, and magical aspects of the yoni.

However you decide to use this arcane knowledge, you do have a moral duty to use it ethically and responsibly. Once again, I must impress upon you that these readings and divinatory rites are not to be performed upon any female under the legal age of consent, nor upon any woman who has been made to assent to a reading or a ritual under duress or while under the influence of intoxicants.

And now, having shared with you the secret divinatory knowledge of a lifetime of personal study, exploration, research, and collaboration with many talented contemporaries and colleagues, I take my leave of you, wishing you all the best.

Dr. Jeremy Weiss

BIBLIOGRAPHY

Allina A. and Ryan K.[Pseud.]. *The Women's Health Activist: Genitally Feminist Healthy.* NWHN.org, 2012.

[Anon.]. *The Flower of Life, The Tree of Life.* StateMaster.com Encyclopedia, 2012.

[Anon.]. *Coitus Reservatus, Female Genital Mutilation, Hymenorrhaphy, Labia Stretching, Paschal Beverly Randolph, Sanitary Napkin, Shakti, Vulva, Yoni.* En.Wikipedia.org, 2014.

Brauer, Allen. *ESO (Extended Sexual Orgasm).* Warner Books, 1984.

Brown, N. *Vaginal Discharge.* Palo Alto Medical Foundation, PAMF.org, 2013.

Burr, Timothy. *BISBA (Burr Identification System of Breast Analysis): Bearing the Breast's Intriguing Mysteries.* Hercules Publishing Company, 1965.

Burton, Natasha. *Six Vaginal Odors to Put On Your Radar.* WomansDay.com, 2015.

Camphausen, Rufus C. *The Yoni: Sacred Symbol of Female Creative Power.* Inner Traditions, 1996.

Clint, Edward. *The Clitoris Revealed and How i09 Got it Wrong.* SkepticInk.com, 2013.

Cyber Docta [Pseud.]. *Can Hymen Regenerate?* Answers.Yahoo.com, 2009.

Dadzie, Sally Kenneth. *It Is Supposed to Smell Like a Vagina!* 360nobs.com, 2014.

Dickinson, Robert Latou. *Human Sex Anatomy: A Topographical Hand Atlas.* Williams & Wilkins, 1949.

Douglas, Nik and Slinger, Penny. *Sexual Secrets: The Alchemy of Ecstasy.* Destiny, 1989.

Flowinglife, Flowguide [Pseud.]. *Tantric Ritual.* Tantra.Flowguide.com, [nd].

Gimbutas, Marija. *The Gods and Goddesses of Old Europe, 7000 - 3500 BC.* University of California Press, 1974.

Hænke, David and Yronwode, Catherine. *Karezza: Victorian Tantra.* New Age Magazine, July 1977.

Heidi [Pseud.]. *What is Neotantra?* HealersWorldwide.com, 2011.

Highbaugh, Kurt. *The Esoteric Codex: Numerology.* Lulu, 2015.

Hillard, Paula J. Adams. *Medscape: Imperforate Hymen Treatment & Management Emedicine.* Medscape.com, 2016.

Him and Her [Pseud.]. *Genital Piercing.* HimAndHerSex.Wordpress.com, 2012.

Howard, Clifford. *Sex Worship.* [-] 1898; 5th ed. Chicago Medical Book Company, 1909.

[Jennings, Hargrave]. *Nature Worship: An Account of Phallic Faiths and Practices, Ancient and Modern, Including the Adoration of the Male and Female Powers in Various Nations and the Sacti Puja of Indian Gnosticism.* Privately printed, 1891.

[Jennings, Hargrave]. *Phallic Miscellanies: Facts and Phases of Ancient and Modern Sex Worship, as Explained Chiefly in the Religions of India.* Privately printed, 1891.

Jennings, Hargrave. *Phallicism, Celestial and Terrestrial, Heathen and Christian, Its Connexion with the Rosicrucians and the Gnostics, and Its Foundation in Buddhism.* George Redway, 1884.

Joy [Pseud.]. *From Dye Bath to Walnut Ink.* JoybileeFarm.com, 2012.

Johnson, Julie Ann. *More Secret Knowledge.* The Private Press, 2009.

Kamalak N., *SlideShare: Episiotomy.* SlideShare.net, 2013.
Kalyana Malla [trans. by Forster Fitzgerald Arbuthnot and Sir Richard Burton]. *Ananga-Ranga, Stage of the Bodiless One or, The Hindu Art of Love.* Kama Shastra Society, 1885.
Lippy Girl [Pseud.] *What is a Hottentot Apron?* HottentotApron.blogspot.com, 2012.
Lloyd, John William. *The Karezza Method; or, Magnetation; the Art of Connubial Love.* Privately Printed for the Author and His Friends, [nd; ca.1917-1918].
Manha, Vinaya Katoch. *Dreaming of Walnuts.* TribuneIndia.com, 2002.
Mazo, Ruth. *What's Up, G? See You at the Spot.* RuthMazo.com, 2013.
May, Andrew. *Mathematics and Mysticism.* Aquarian Newsletter, February, 2006.
Melodious Ms M. [Pseud.] *MoSex Blog: The Internal Clitoris.* MoSex.Wordpress.com, 2011.
Miller, George Noyes. *The Strike of a Sex and Zugassent's Discovery or, After the Sex Struck.* Stockham Publishing Co., 1905.
Mookerjie, Ajit. *Kali: The Feminine Force.* Thames and Hudson/Destiny Books, 1988.
Morris, Ceridwen. *The "Husband's Stitch": Unnecessary Episiotomies.* Babble.com, 2013.
Muir, Charles and Muir, Caroline. *Tantra: The Art of Conscious Loving.* Mercury House, 1989.
Netter, Frank Henry and Oppenheimer, Ernst. *The Ciba Collection of Medical Illustrations.* Vol. 2: Reproductive System. Ciba, 1954. Online at DocIn.com/p-333382451.html.
Newton, A. E. *The Better Way: An Appeal to Men.* Wood and Holbrook, 1875.
Olschewski, Martha. *Genital Horoscope.* AstroGenital.com, 1998.
Ramsdale, David and Ramsdale, Ellen. *Sexual Energy Ecstasy.* Bantam, 1985.
Randolph, Paschal Beverly. *Eulis! The History of Love: Its Wondrous Magic, Chemistry, Rules, Laws, Modes, Moods and Rationale.* [Randolph Publishing Co.], 1874
Rankin, Lissa. *How are Vaginas Supposed to Smell?* BlogHer.com, 2010.
Rawson, Philip. *Tantra: The Indian Cult of Ecstasy.* Thames and Hudson, 1973.
Savory, George W. *Hell Upon Earth Made Heaven.* Order of the Orange Blossom, 1905.
Schwartz, Bob. *The One Hour Orgasm.* Breakthru Publishing, 1988.
Stockham, Alice Bunker. *Karezza: Ethics of Marriage.* R. F. Fenno & Co., 1896.
Stubbs, Kenneth Ray. *Sensual Ceremony: A Contemporary Tantric Guide to Sexual Intimacy.* Secret Garden Publishing, 1992.
Symonds, R. *How the Vesica Pisces Explains Creation.* EzineArticles.com, 2010.
Vatsayana [trans. by Forster Fitzgerald Arbuthnot and Sir Richard Burton]. *The Kama Sutra of Vatsayana, in Seven Parts.* The Hindoo Kama Shastra Society, 1883.
Wile, Douglas. *Art of the Bedchamber: Chinese Sexual Yoga Classics.* SUNY Press, 1992.
Wonkette [Pseud]. *Please Buy Us This Artificial Hymen So We Can Be Pure Again.* Wonkette.com, 2014.
Yoniversity. *The Yoni.* Yoniversum.nl/yoni/yonilist.html, 1996.
Yronwode, Althæa. *Study Claims Clitoris Larger Than Thought.* LuckyMojo.com, 1999.
Yronwode, Catherine. *Sacred Sex: The Biological Basis of Sacred Sex, Body Fluids in Hoodoo, Karezza Techniques, Paschal Beverley Randolph.* LuckyMojo.com. 1995 - 2017.
Yronwode, Catherine. *Throwing the Bones.* Lucky Mojo Curio Co., 2012.
Zimmer, Heinrich. *Myths and Symbols in Indian Art and Civilization.* Princeton Press, 1972.